Gaza Envelope

OCTOBER 7
Hamas against Israel

The Myths
The Propaganda
The Truth

Ernesto Katzenstein

English language editor: Tim Houghton

VAKTEL BOOKS

This book is dedicated to the Palestinian and foreign journalists who have reported from the Occupied Territories for decades at the risk of their lives; and especially to the victims of Israel's bombing of Gaza.

Vaktel
förlag

Vaktel Books
vaktelforlag.se
forlag@vaktelforlag.se

Table of contents

In few national conflicts has propaganda become such a poisonous weapon and achieved such a powerful hold over the minds of leaders and people alike. Partisanship, emotional bias and propaganda pervade the massive literature on the Israeli-Arab conflict and have created a thick fog obscuring its real content. Arguments advanced in the heat of passionate debate and in the struggle to gain support of public opinion at home and abroad have acquired the status and force of axioms and absolute truths. While statesmen have become prisoners of their own propaganda, the peoples have become its victims.
    – Simha Faplan, *Zionism and the Palestinians, 1979*

The furious reactions to even the slightest criticism actually make one suspect that some Israelis may, deep down in their hardened hearts, know that something terrible is burning under their feet, that a huge fire is threatening to break through the thick, stupefying, distorting and bewildering fog that lies over them. If Israelis were really so convinced of the rightness of their cause, why the violent intolerance of anyone who tries to argue otherwise?
    – Gideon Levy, *Gaza, My Beloved, 2010*

Some of the Zionists leaders pretend to believe that the Jews can maintain themselves in Palestine against the whole world and that they themselves can persevere in claiming everything or nothing against everybody and everything. However, behind this spurious optimism lurks a despair of everything and a genuine readiness for suicide that can become extremely dangerous should they grow to be the mood and atmosphere of Palestinian politics.
    – Hannah Arendt, *The Jewish State: Fifty Years After, Where Have Herzl's Politics Led?, 1947*

Glossary

al-Aqsa – A mosque on the Temple Mount (Haram al-Sharif) in Old Jerusalem, opposite the Dome of the Rock (the one with the golden dome).

al-Aqsa Brigades – Fatah's armed wing is called the al-Aqsa Martyrs' Brigade.

Al Quds – the Arabic name for Jerusalem.

al Quds Brigades – the armed wing of Islamic Jihad.

Ashkenazi – Jews from Germany. Started appearing in the German-Roman Empire around 1000 AD and spread in Eastern and Northern Europe. In Eastern Europe they spoke Yiddish. The Israeli political, economic, and cultural elite are mainly Ashkenazi. The other groups – *Sephardim*, *Mizrahim*, Yemenites, and Ethiopian Jews have been more or less discriminated against.

Eretz Israel – the land of Israel in Hebrew. It is sometimes referred to as Greater Israel. Most consider it to include the area that was part of the former British Mandate of Palestine (Mandatory Palestine or Historic Palestine), from the Jordan River to the Mediterranean Sea (the territory today effectively controlled by Israel). Some groups claim that parts of Syria, Lebanon, Jordan, and Egypt are also part of Eretz Israel.

Fatah – the Palestinian National Liberation Movement, founded in exile, originally with a nationalist and left ideology. The party of Yasser Arafat, now led by Mahmoud Abbas (abu Mazen), Fatah is the largest group within the PLO.

Gaza Envelope – the string of Israeli communities and military posts surrounding the Gaza Strip.

Green Line – the border of the State of Israel after the 1949 armistice. Covers 78% of historic Palestine.

Haganah – the Jewish militias during the British Mandate in Palestine (1922–1948). Led by David Ben Gurion who was the leader of the Social Democratic Party (Labour) and became the first Prime Minister of Israel.

Hamas – Islamic Resistance Movement, founded in 1987 from the Islamic Society, a charitable organization operating in the occupied territories; founded in 1969, as a section of the Muslim Brotherhood (an Egyptian religious movement founded in the 1920s).

IDF – Israeli Defence Forces, the Israeli army.

Irgun – a guerrilla group that grew out of Zionist revisionism. Led by Menachem Begin, the British classified them as terrorists and Begin was a wanted man.

Kibbutz – a Jewish Israeli community in the countryside. At the beginning of the Jewish colonization of Palestine, the kibbutz was a kind of collective communist society, with a communal dining room, child rearing, etc. Today, this collective aspect is greatly reduced. The country's 267 kibbutzim account for 1.7 percent of Israel's population. For a time, going to work on a kibbutz was popular among Western youth.

Knesset – the Israeli parliament consists of 120 members, currently from 11 parties. Netanyahu's Likud party is the largest party with 32 members.

Lehi (Stern League) – a breakaway group from the Irgun, and like it, classified as a terrorist group by the British. Led by Yitzhak Shamir, later Prime Minister of Israel.

Mizrahim – Oriental Jews who lived in Arab countries and Iran (there is still a small group of Jews in Iran and other countries). The vast majority migrated to Israel in the late 1940s and early 1950s.

Magen David Adom – the Israeli Red Cross.

Moshav – a kind of agricultural cooperative for small farmers in Israel.

Mossad – Israeli intelligence service, Israel's CIA. The country's central agency for intelligence and special missions abroad.

Nakba – the word means catastrophe in Arabic and refers to the violent campaign waged by the Jewish militias Haganah, Palmach, Irgun, and Lehi between 1947 and 1949, which left thousands of Palestinians dead, emptied over 530 villages and communities of their inhabitants, and displaced 80% of Palestinians (in the territories that became the state of Israel) from their villages and towns into neighboring countries. Since then, they have been forbidden by Israel to return to their land.

Nukhba – Qassam brigades elite soldiers.

Oslo Agreement – The Oslo Agreement was signed by Yasser Arafat and Yitzhak Rabin at the White House in 1993. Israel recognized the PLO as the legitimate representative of the Palestinian people and the PLO recognized Israel within the 1967 borders (Green Line). The Palestinian Authority was established as the embryo of the Palestinian state that would be proclaimed 5 years later. Arafat and some other Palestinian leaders were allowed into Gaza and the West Bank, but not the Palestinian refugees in neighboring countries. Hamas interpreted the Oslo Agreement as a trap and opposed it.

PA or Palestinian Authority – the administration set up by the Oslo Accords, which would eventually become the State of Palestine. Over time, the Palestinian Authority has become more and more an administrator of the occupation on behalf of Israel. A large proportion of Palestinians believe it should be dissolved.

Palmach – Haganah elite troops.

Partition Plan – Decision 181 of the UN General Assembly adopted on November 29, 1947. The territory of the British Mandate was to be divided and two states were to be created: a Jewish state on 55% and an Arab state on 45% of the territory.

PLO – Palestine Liberation Organization – Palestinian umbrella organization founded in 1964 in exile, recognized as a UN observer in 1974. The PLO constituted the Palestinian Authority.

Qassam – Izz ad-Din al-Qassam was a Syrian Muslim preacher and a leader in the Arab nationalist struggles against British and French in the Levant and a militant opponent of Zionism in the 1920s and 1930s, killed in 1935 by the British.

Qassam Brigades – the armed wing of Hamas.

RPG – Rocket Propelled Grenade – originally a Soviet rocket launcher. Hamas has developed the RPG and manufactures the RPG itself, called the Yassin-2 and Yassin-7.

Red Crescent – the Muslim Red Cross.

Sephardic Jews – Jews from the Iberian Peninsula, Spain, and Portugal (Sepharad in Hebrew). Like most European countries, Spain expelled the Jews. In 1492, the last city held by the Arabs in southern Spain, Granada, fell. Along with the Arabs, the Jews were expelled and spread throughout the Mediterranean, as far as the Balkan Peninsula and North Africa.

Shin Bet – the Israeli security police.

Ulama – 'those who possess knowledge', a term for religious scholars in Islam.

Ummah – the community of believers in Islam.

YAMAM – also known as the Anti-Terrorism Unit, part of the Border Police in Israel.

Yassin – Ahmed Yassin (1936–2004), founder of Hamas, who was also a spiritual leader.

Zionism – the ideology that advocates the creation of a Jewish state in Palestine. Hungarian journalist Theodor Herzl founded the movement, which first met in Basel in 1897. Initially, Zionism was secular. In the 1920s, Zeev Jabotinsky founded a more radical tendency, Revisionism, from which Netanyahu's Likud party was formed.

Preface

For a few months in 2011, I was in Palestine and Israel as an accompanier as part of the Ecumenical Accompaniment Program in Palestine and Israel (EAPPI) run by the World Council of Churches, based in Tulkarm in the northwestern West Bank. Afterwards, I met with friends and relatives in Israel.

As we walked in the park by the seashore in Old Jaffa my friend GL, professor at Tel Aviv university, pointed to the sea and the rocks: "A hundred years ago, many Zionists came from Europe. The boats could not reach the shore and they were carried to the mainland by the Palestinians on their backs. Maybe Ben Gurion was one of them."

GL recounted the brutal expulsion of Palestinians from Jaffa during the Nakba of 1948–1949.

"The State of Israel was founded on the ruins of the Palestinian society, a catastrophe. Now must we, our generation, resolve the situation without causing a new catastrophe".

A few days later I was with some acquaintances in Tel Aviv. A couple of them eagerly asked how things were in "the territories", as Israelis call the occupied territories. Why don't you go there yourself, I asked, it's only an hour away. There are buses from Jerusalem to Ramallah. Nothing difficult.

They shook their heads in resignation and kept asking. They were honestly curious, and I realized they knew nothing about how Palestinians lived in the territories their country occupies. Although they were critical of the occupation, I realized that they were unable to break the many written and unwritten rules that govern life in Israel (Israeli citizens are prohibited by Israeli law from visiting the main Palestinian cities – Area A under the Oslo Accords). The uncertainty and fear of the 'Arab' was perhaps greater than the curiosity.

This little book has modest aims: to distinguish things from people, to clarify what we know and what we don't know about what happened, and to open doors to understanding why Hamas and Israel act as they do – before, during and after the October 7 attack, which Hamas calls the *Al-Aqsa flood* and which Israel calls the *Black Sabbath*. In the war zone, lives are at stake every second, but an equally important and fierce battle is going on outside. A battle for the truth that is waged with words and images on TV and the internet, in newspapers and magazines.

We need to distinguish between things and people because we are all caught in linguistic traps, even prisons. The first is the word *terrorist*. A trap? Yes, because cataloging a person or group as a terrorist means, for most of us, more or less consciously, that everything that group or person does is an act of terrorism. The word terrorist frees us from further investigation. A terrorist, person, or group is a destructive nihilist, incapable not only of good deeds, but also of acting rationally, one who is driven solely by negative, low, primitive emotions such as hatred, contempt, and revenge, who cannot empathize or understand the perspectives and needs of other people. In a fight between a terrorist and any other person, group, society, state, it is obvious which side is the right one.

September 11, 2001, buried the somewhat idyllic post-Cold War period when Clinton and Yeltsin danced and laughed together. The new century and millennium started with the "war on terror". Before, the terrorist was a guerrilla man or woman hiding in the forests or mountains of South America – a child of Che Guevara's guerrillas – or a Palestinian from Black September who hijacks an airplane or kills Israelis. But now the terrorist has become a caricature of the terrorist. He has grown a beard, donned a turban and loose, foot-long tunics, kneeling in the direction of Mecca, and shouting Allahu Akbar as he attacks beautiful, civilized, white, Christian people. His whole environment has become part of him. His women, for example, have hijabs on their heads, even in modern cities. Religion has taken over and he has become a fundamentalist.

Now you are, I suppose, upset and thinking: *Stop, I don't think like that. You are describing prejudiced, ignorant people.*

Sure, sure. But neither you nor I can completely free ourselves from that pesky little doubt that still swims in our brains. Okay, maybe not with you, but at least with me, that little suspicion is always there. Well, you know… Mmm… the Muslims… Arab men, yes…

An obvious risk is to become resigned. Israel and Palestine have fought all these years and will continue to do so. They both commit crimes, they're cut from the same cloth. But I have a few objections: first, they are not two equal parties – and, as Teddy Bear, or whoever it was, said, if you are strong, you have to be nice. Second, this book will show that one side systematically lies and uses false propaganda that appeals to emotions and prejudices. And third, we must not forget that the Jews lived in peace in the region we call the Middle East throughout the long period when they were persecuted, discriminated against, and expelled from one country after another by Christian Europe, culminating in the Nazi attempt to eradicate European Jewry during the Holocaust – which is certainly not to say that the Holocaust was inevitable.

If you're going to read this book, you have to make a deal with me: we have to forget the stamps and labels and together try to dispel the fog, make an effort to find out what we really know about what happened on October 7, 2023, what led up to it and what happened after it, and try to analyze the motives behind it. It may sound simple, but it may require an almost superhuman effort. It will require patience and you will have to succeed in suppressing spontaneous thoughts (call it prejudice if you like) and try to ignore the massive propaganda that washes over us and obfuscates our thoughts and minds.

I will be careful with the use of adjectives, and I will not begin with the ritual that seems to be required of anyone who wants to say anything at all on the issue: condemn Hamas's brutal murders, violence, and ruthlessness, "heinous crimes", etc. Nor will I denounce on every page Israel's bombing of Gaza or oppression in the West Bank.

It is remarkable how even serious organizations rushed to condemn Hamas for killing 1,400 civilians and committing crimes such as rape before there was even proof of the number of dead or who had killed them, while not a word was said about the perhaps up to three thousand people from Gaza, far from all of whom were members of the al-Qassam Brigades (Hamas's armed wing), who were killed that day.

The polarization of the media climate has reached unprecedented heights. Media critic Sana Saeed told *The Intercept* on October 11, 2023: "We have seen journalists, in particular, spread unverified information that is being used to justify Israeli and even American calls and actions to annihilate an entire population."[1] Therefore, I choose to remain as neutral as possible and limit myself to presenting the facts of what happened on October 7 so that you, the reader, can draw your own conclusions.

The first part of this work is devoted to trying to understand why so many people died on October 7. Later on, the motives behind the actions of the different parties are analyzed. I try to keep my reasoning as free as possible from emotions and moral constraints, because an objective analysis of the facts and the motives is important to assess what happened. In the last part, some elements to understand the background of the current conflict are briefly presented.

There are undoubtedly situations where war and violence are justified, fair, and even absolutely necessary and inevitable. But we must not forget that all wars are brutal events and in all wars all sides commit abuses. This is not an excuse. Crimes and abuses, war crimes and crimes against humanity must be investigated and punished regardless of who commits them.

The authors of the laws of war (the Geneva Conventions) were not hypocritical moralists but understood that in war the innocent are caught in the middle and suffer greatly. The Conventions do not condemn all "collateral damage" but set clear limits; unfortunately, in recent decades we have seen this abused.

It has been difficult for me to question the stories of people who have been exposed to great danger and horror. I want to feel, and I do feel solidarity with the victims, whoever they are, but I had to analyse the testimonies and compare them to other stories. It was hard to question the testimony of a man who filmed events in a small, crowded bomb shelter next to a bus stop, who was terrified when militiamen or Palestinian civilians tossed grenades into the shelter; and I want to comfort him when he says he can't walk because the muscles of one of his legs was ripped off by the shell; but when a minute later he says he escaped death by hiding under the bodies and body parts of the dead, I start to wonder, especially as I hear the interviewer whispering to the young man. When I read exactly the same words from several witnesses who were in other similar shelters, I have to ask myself some questions.

What does a terrorist look like?

A journalist from the Israeli newspaper *Haaretz* wrote, referring to Hamas militiamen: "a jihadist fighter is a rather dangerous combination: a professional soldier who is eager to die".[2] Is this the case with Hamas militiamen? That they are prepared to die cannot be questioned. Hamas has used suicide bombers and attacks where the perpetrator knows with almost 100% certainty that they will die. But does this mean that they are nihilistic, absurd, tragic figures who want to die? Or should we understand it to be the same case as with most guerrilla and liberation movements, that the fighters are aware of the risks, but that doesn't mean they want to die?

It was when a suicide bomber took the life of his niece that Miko Peled's curiosity was aroused, leading him – the son of a general in the Israeli army during the 6-Day War, and the grandson of one of the founders of the State of Israel – to become a staunch defender of the Palestinian struggle. Similarly, Bernt Hermele tried to find an explanation for the murder of his mother in a suicide attack in Israel. What could lead a person to do something as seemingly irrational and desperate as sacrificing their own life?[3]

Hamas communiqués during the war have usually ended with the statement "the soldiers returned to their bases unharmed", indicating an interest in preserving their troops. And how to interpret Menachem Begin, the leader of the Irgun urban guerrillas during the British mandate in the 1930s and 1940s, when he says: "There is a life that is worse than death and a death that is better than life."[4]

Who deserves to be called a terrorist? Is it possible to come up with a definition? What is the opposite of a terrorist? And above all, who are the judges who decide whether you should or should not be labelled a terrorist? The EU and the US, but not the rest of the world, have labelled Hamas a terrorist organization, while much of the Arab world and the countries of the "Global South" (and some scholars in academia) see it as a liberation movement.

Menachem Begin, who became Prime Minister of Israel, called Yasser Arafat and the Palestinians "a beast on two legs". The British classified Begin's Irgun as a terrorist organization, and he was a wanted man. In 1951 he published *The Revolt*, a book that was used by Marxist urban guerrilla movements in South America in the 1960s because the book was like an instruction manual for urban guerrilla warfare. The Irgun carried out several terrorist acts, including the bombing of the King David Hotel in central Jerusalem that killed nearly one hundred people. In his book, Begin wrote:

… our enemies called us terrorists. Some who were neither friends nor enemies, such as correspondents of the New York Herald Tribune, also used this Latin word, influenced by the British or by habit… [others] called us murderers, criminals.

When Begin visited the United States, several Jewish personalities, including Hannah Arendt and Albert Einstein, wrote an open letter to the editor of The New York Times[5] (1948-12-04) to protest that people who supported the fight against fascism could support Mr. Begin. They did not mince words:

Among the most disturbing political phenomena of our times is the emergence in the newly created state of Israel of the "Freedom Party" (Tnuat Haherut), a political party closely akin in its organization, methods, political philosophy and social appeal to the Nazi and Fascist parties. It was formed out of the membership and following of the former Irgun Zvai Leumi, a terrorist, right-wing, chauvinist organization in Palestine. [...]

Today they speak of freedom, democracy and anti-imperialism, whereas until recently they openly preached the doctrine of the Fascist state. It is in its actions that the terrorist party betrays its real character; from its past actions we can judge what it may be expected to do in the future.

Lehi (Stern League) was a breakaway group from the Irgun led by Yitzhak Shamir (who also became Prime Minister of Israel in the 1980s). Lehi was also classified as a terrorist organization; during the British Mandate period, they murdered several people and carried out attacks both in Palestine and abroad, most notably the assassination of the British Governor Lord Moyne in Cairo in 1944, an attack on the British Embassy in Rome, and the assassination of UN mediator Folke Bernadotte in Jerusalem in 1948 – as he was about to present a plan that included the return of Palestinian refugees.[6]

After September 11, 2001, the word terrorist has been linked to other old collective notions of the Arab, the Oriental, the Mujahideen. The terrorist changed names a few times but has been crystallized over the past two decades in the equation: *terrorist = IS*, which somewhere in our collective reptilian brain emerges as a blurred image of a rider at a gallop with his scimitar ready to cut off the head of anyone who gets in his way. When someone commits an indiscriminate act – bombing, killing, maiming, the media has no problem calling him a terrorist if he comes from the ill-defined area known as "the Middle East" but quite a bit of trouble using the same word if he is a white, Christian, Western, well, "ordinary" person.

There is no reason to believe that a terrorist can only be a person or a group. We tend to see the state as legitimate. A state can make mistakes; state officials, police, and authorities can abuse their power, be corrupt, and commit abuses. But *we always see the state as legitimate*. It can make mistakes, but the state as such cannot, by definition, be wrong. Of course, this is not the case. The states that exist today didn't always exist, and some of them probably won't last – they will merge with others or break up when citizens think it's time for change, or they change their constitution and rules and become another state. States are not eternal beings. And, more importantly, even states use terrorism and practice state terrorism and may need to be changed, even buried, and replaced by another. The most obvious example, but far from the only one, was Germany under Hitler. In the conflict we are dealing with here, we tend to think that Israel commits atrocities, well, who doesn't? – but Hamas (and the Palestinians), well, they engage in terrorism.

Ronen Bergman has written a book[7] about Israel's use of targeted killings. After World War II, some secret agents hunted down and killed Nazis in Germany until the British protested – you couldn't do justice that way. Then they targeted a German colony in Tel Aviv, Haifa, and the Galilee, and the Germans left Palestine. Sometime after this campaign, Ben Gurion approved their methods: targeted killings, guerrilla warfare, terrorist attacks.

Most liberation movements have used guerrilla methods and terror (the weapon of the weak, as Avi Shlaim puts it in a forthcoming book), which usually ends when the goal is achieved (often the liberation from a foreign occupation). But in the case of Israel, this does not seem to be the case. Bergman's book shows that the state of Israel deliberately practiced terror and committed terrorist acts. How does it work to accuse others of terror when you consider yourself entitled to use the same methods? What does that do to a person?

The guerrillas changed and became a state which did not renounce to practice terror when it considered it justified. But we do not call Israel a terrorist state. Israeli journalist and author Ronen Bergman writes in his book *Rise and Kill First*:

> *"The Holocaust taught the Jews that they will always be under the threat of annihilation, that others cannot be trusted to protect the Jews. A people who live under the sense of perpetual danger of annihilation will resort to any measure, no matter how extreme, to ensure safety, and will adhere to international laws and regulations at the margins, if at all.*

Is this still the case today? Does Israel "adhere to international laws and rules at the margin, if at all"? Did they stop being terrorists?

The British claimed in the early 20th century that the Arabs understood only violence and terror, and coined the words "terror bombing" during the war in Iraq in the 1920s. Jonathan Glancey wrote in The Guardian in 2003:[8]

Churchill was particularly keen on chemical weapons, suggesting they be used 'against recalcitrant Arabs as an experiment'. He dismissed objections as 'unreasonable'. 'I am strongly in favour of using poisoned gas against uncivilised tribes... [to] spread a lively terror ...' In today's terms, 'the Arab' needed to be shocked and awed. A good gassing might well do the job. Conventional raids, however, proved to be an effective deterrent. They brought Sheikh Mahmoud, the most persistent of Kurdish rebels, to heel, at little cost.

Writing in 1921, Wing Commander J A Chamier suggested that the best way to demoralise local people was to concentrate bombing on the 'most inaccessible village of the most prominent tribe which it is desired to punish. All available aircraft must be collected, the attack with bombs and machine guns must be relentless and unremitting and carried on continuously by day and night, on houses, inhabitants, crops and cattle.'

'The Arab and Kurd now know', reported Squadron Leader Harris after several such raids, 'what real bombing means. Within 45 minutes a full-sized village can be practically wiped out, and a third of its inhabitants killed or injured, by four or five machines which offer them no real target, no opportunity for glory as warriors, no effective means of escape.'

In his memoir of the crushing of the 1920 Iraqi uprising, Lieutenant-General Sir Aylmer L Haldane, quotes his own orders for the punishment of any Iraqi found in possession of weapons 'with the utmost severity': 'The village where he resides will be destroyed ... pressure will be brought on the inhabitants by cutting off water, power, the area being cleared of the necessaries of life'. He added the warning: 'Burning a village properly takes a long time, an hour or more according to size'.

Who is the terrorist? What does he look like?

What happened on October 7?

You have a choice: when you learn of the horrors which humans are capable of inflicting against each other you either allow these Horrors to deepen your Humanity or you use those Horrors to numb your Humanity so that you can be complicit in even more and indeed often greater horrors.

– Owen Jones, 2023-11-27, *I Watched The Hamas Massacre Film. Here Are My Thoughts*, after watching the IDF film aimed at exposing Hamas's actions.

The world was shaken by the attack on October 7, 2023. Prime Minister Netanyahu spoke of beheaded children, raped women, horrific massacres, and bloodthirsty murderers the world had never seen before. The media in the US, the EU, Sweden, and many other countries spread this horrifying image; the US and EU governments echoed it and expressed their disgust, while photographs and videos of dead people, burnt cars and destroyed buildings spread across the world. At the same time, we saw images of Hamas militia men flying over the Gaza wall in paragliders, while excavators tore down fences or smashed the wall, and people poured through into Israel.

On October 12, Amnesty International published a report denouncing Hamas for "deliberate civilian killings, abductions and indiscriminate attacks" and on October 18, Human Rights Watch[9] published three videos showing the killing of civilians by Hamas militiamen and others without uniforms and called for the International Criminal Court (ICC) to investigate the crimes committed that day.

The assault began with massive rocket attacks from Gaza against communities in the *Gaza Envelope*, the string of kibbutzim, communities, and military bases that surround the narrow strip, as well as Tel Aviv, Jerusalem, and Ben Gurion airport.

The media described it as a bloody, unnecessary, absurd massacre with no other purpose than killing for the sake of killing, a "vengeful pathology"[10] that drove "hate merchants",[11] "worse than ISIS". In Germany and France, pro-Palestinian protesters were met with tear gas or imprisoned. In the UK, protesters against the bombing of Gaza were called terrorists by government officials. The White House press secretary distanced himself from some members of Congress, saying it was wrong, unfortunate, and repugnant to call for a ceasefire; in Sweden the leader of the Swedish Democrats (far right wing) suggested on Swedish Radio that "foreigners celebrating the attacks should be deportable".[12]

A good friend dismissed any discussion: "Israel is a democracy. Hamas is a terrorist organization". For him, that said it all. Another said: "Hamas does not represent the Palestinians". In this way, he wanted to remain neutral, yet he distanced himself from the violence that shocked everyone.

But another interpretation is possible. Let me quote Hanan Ashrawi, a former member of the Palestinian parliament and peace negotiator: the October 7 attack was "an act of resistance against the occupation army".[13] The American scholar Norman Finkelstein[14] compares October 7 to the 1831 slave revolt in the United States, led by Nat Turner, that raised the moral question of the legitimacy of the violence of the slaves versus the violence of the slave owners.

On Wednesday, October 11, 2023, the Israeli government released a video[15] of a phone call between Netanyahu and Biden, in which Netanyahu speaks of hundreds massacred, families wiped out in their beds at home, women brutally raped and murdered, over a hundred kidnapped, including children. He said that since they last spoke, this evil had only gotten worse – "they had taken dozens of children, tied them up, burned them, and executed them. They had beheaded soldiers… they had mowed down young people who had gone to a nature festival, they had placed five jeeps around a depression in the ground and, as in Babi Yar,[16] they had mowed everyone down and made sure they had killed everyone". He said they had never seen such brutality in the history of the state; he claimed they were "worse than ISIS, and that they must be treated accordingly…"

The Netanyahu X account (Twitter) claims that Prime Minister Benjamin Netanyahu showed the pictures to US Secretary of State Antony Blinken. President Biden said: "I have been doing this a long time. I never really thought I would see… confirmed pictures of terrorists beheading children".

Tal Heinrich, a spokeswoman for Netanyahu, said that beheaded babies and toddlers had been found in Kfar Aza and an IDF spokesman, Jonathan Conricus, said, "I think we can now say with relative confidence that unfortunately this is what happened in Be'eri". But the White House was quick to issue a denial: neither the president nor anyone else had seen images of decapitated children. "The Israeli government cannot confirm that babies were beheaded," wrote Matthew Chance, Richard Allen Greene, and Joshua Berlinger on CNN on October 13, 2023.[17]

Owen Jones and the IDF film

Owen Jones is a British journalist who was invited to attend the IDF screening of a film on "Hamas atrocities" on October 7, in Westminster, London. On his YouTube channel[18] he posted a video under the title *"I Watched The Hamas Massacre Film. Here Are My Thoughts"*. The purpose of the IDF film was explicitly to show the horrors of Hamas, but also to make a "PR case for the Israeli onslaught in Gaza". It was "Israel's official story".

But Jones is not uncritical. He notes that the Israeli propaganda film uses the term Judea and Samaria instead of the West Bank, which, Jones comments, "implies an annexation of the West Bank. The film was harrowing to watch, as I expected... Much of what we saw has already gone public and confirms that Hamas has committed war crimes.... Nothing can justify the killing of civilians... You would expect that it was the worst they have to show – this is not a criticism, everyone would do the same". He argues that the material should be given to independent analysts who could go through it, something that should be obvious in any other context.

He also questions whether it is possible to form a complete and fair picture of what is shown in the film: "... a genuinely independent journalist or historian wouldn't conclude they could assess accurately the full nature of what happened on 7th of October from this selection". Jones describes the terrifying scene of a father running with his child and being killed. "Terrible, this will stay with me forever. No question about that." But he also says that in the film, Hamas militiamen in some cases asked whether the people they encountered were soldiers or not – "some kind of consideration seems to have been given to this". (The fact that a quarter of the dead were soldiers does not necessarily mean that they were "legitimate targets". Soldiers who have laid down their arms or been captured are "protected persons" under the Geneva Convention.)

I mention Jones's video here because it is a summary that seems fair and balanced and because he was shown a film that must reasonably be considered the most convincing; and yet he was not convinced. He repeatedly says that there can be no doubt that Hamas committed war crimes and brutal acts, but he also says that some allegations that have been circulating are unsubstantiated (including rapes and 40 beheaded children). The IDF had taken many body cameras off the bodies of Hamas combatants, but when asked why no evidence of these abuses had been shown, the answer was that it was not possible because of the need to protect privacy, and that Hamas had not filmed these abuses. Jones says that this is still surprising because there were lots of CCTV and surveillance cameras at the sites of the attacks. The film claims to have intercepted conversations between Hamas men and their families in which they celebrated the massacres in brutal, sadistic terms, saying they were instructed to behead people and play football with their heads. The IDF has also made similar claims in the past, Jones says, and these recordings have been questioned by the technicians who analyzed them.

What particularly shocked Jones was that the video was compiled to gain support for Israel's bombing campaign against Gaza, which he strongly opposes.

Jones concludes by recounting some brutal abuses during the Balkan war that he reported on – committed not by Serbs but by Muslim Bosniaks and Croats. Would it have been legitimate, he asks rhetorically, to use these atrocities in a propaganda film to justify the atrocities committed by the Bosnian Serbs against the Bosniaks? The most brutal atrocities, he concludes, are committed by people who help the aunt across the street, feel sorrow and joy; ordinary people. Like you and me.

Call for an official commission of inquiry

One characteristic of the edited images and presentations in the major media (*CNN*, *ABC*, *New York Times*, etc.) is that many images do not match the written text or what the journalist says. Another feature is that the presentations warn viewers about disturbing images, but the images shown are not disturbing – just people running or standing, empty and destroyed cars and houses. Furthermore, the masking of individuals is overused. Masking is necessary to protect individuals, but in many cases, it is not possible to assess whether what is shown lying on the ground is a body or something else.

Some of the allegations are arguably so extreme as to be absurd, such as the claim that football was played with heads of beheaded people, or the bestial abuse of women, raped and mutilated, with their breasts cut off and their entrails scattered around. Brutality against babies, children, and women is particularly effective in arousing emotional reactions and blinding the public. See Appendix III, section "Atrocity Propaganda", page XXX.

Rectifications usually follow, but far from always, and do not receive as much media coverage. Rectifications target the brain of the reader or viewer, while the emotions evoked by the original news story often remain. Not without reason; such accusations, despite denials, are consistently repeated. It seems to be an application of what is known as *point scoring*, in pro-Israel Zionist propaganda manuals:[19] "Point scoring communication ought to give the appearance of rational debate, whilst avoiding genuine discussion… Point scoring works because most audience members fail to analyse what they hear. Rather, they register only a few key points, and form a vague impression of whose 'argument' was stronger. Point scoring is the correct method of communication to use when the audience is likely to be only partially engaged."

A writer in Israel, who wishes to remain anonymous for fear of reprisals, wrote in *Mondoweiss*[20] on October 22, 2023, that "it will take years until we may (or may not) have a full picture of what happened on October 7 and the following days." He wrote that the Israeli army was responsible for many of the deaths on October 7 and mentioned the Hannibal Directive as a possible explanation. The information about what took place was so contradictory that a group of Israeli citizens wrote an open letter demanding an independent investigation. *Mondoweiss* published the letter in English and Hebrew on October 31, 2023:[21]

Make no mistake, what Israel is doing in Gaza now will haunt Israelis for decades. Now is the time to make sure all Israelis understand this. And this understanding should start with full disclosure about the events of October 7, 2023.

Here are a few demands that each Israeli should be making right now, even if they deny the ongoing Gaza genocide. The first one is a comprehensive list of all the Israeli victims who have been identified. There is no comprehensive list on an official government website. The list published by Haaretz is partial. Some names are waiting to be 'cleared for publication', and we would like to know what this means.

The lack of a comprehensive list, three weeks in, leads to the next demand Israeli citizens must make — the establishment of an official investigation commission. Massive failures on the part of intelligence and combat units, as well as the Israeli insistence on turning Gaza into an open-air prison in the preceding decades, should obviously be addressed by such a commission. We would like to know how these failures contributed to civilian fatalities on October 7 and the following days. […]

And while our military exterminates human beings in Gaza, Israeli Hasbara (propaganda) platforms are in overdrive, especially abroad. The charred remains[22] of loved ones are paraded around, nameless, contextualized only by dehumanizing calls to eradicate the inmates of the Gaza concentration camp. Upon seeing these images, aimed at a Western audience and with complete disregard for survivors' families, we note once more that all of us deserve precise information as to who these victims are and how they died.

Conspiracy theories and lies –
Hamas massacre denials

This headline opened an article by Sagi Cohen in the Israeli newspaper *Haaretz* on November 7: "Conspiracy theories and lies – denials of the October 7 Hamas massacre are gaining ground online".[23]

> *The false posts mix lies and baseless allegations – against the backdrop of antisemitism and anti-Israel stances. Conspiracy theorists don't claim that the entire event was fabricated, but they say the death toll is much lower than reported. They argue that Hamas didn't plan to kill civilians and mainly targeted soldiers, that atrocities such as rape and beheadings didn't take place, and that most of the civilians murdered were actually killed in an exchange of fire or by the Israeli army … The deniers completely ignore the plethora of videos and photos showing that Hamas murdered Israelis and burned their houses.*

The author mentions references to the Hannibal Directive, which was cancelled by the then-Chief of Staff, Gadi Eisenkot in 2016.

> *Like other fake news campaigns, these theories rely on snippets of evidence while completely ignoring anything that contradicts them. One video that went viral claims that all the deaths at Kibbutz Be'eri were the work of Israeli tanks that lost control and simply shelled houses.*

The same newspaper, *Haaretz*, published, a month later, on December 4, 2023, an article by Nir Hasson and Liza Rozovsky[24] which argues that "The extensive evidence of crimes against humanity committed by Hamas terrorists on October 7 should not be contaminated by unverified stories disseminated by Israeli search and rescue groups, army officers and even Sara Netanyahu [...] Most [atrocities committed by Hamas] are supported by extensive evidence, but a few have been proved untrue, providing ammunition to deniers of the historic massacre." The authors of the article refer to a post[25] on *i24NEWS*, an Israeli news channel, with the headline, "Watch Now: Beheaded Babies and Women Found in Kfar Aza", in which an army officer said that "at least 40 babies have been killed, some of them decapitated". The Israeli Foreign Ministry published the information from Colonel Golan Vach, Home Front Commando, who claimed that he "found the bodies of eight burned babies in a house". *Haaretz's* article mentions Ishay Coen, a journalist at the ultra-Orthodox website *Kikar*

Hashabbat, who quotes Lieutenant Colonel Yaron Buskila of the IDF's Gaza Division: "Buskila talked about babies who had been hung on clotheslines; his remarks were cited by a host of Twitter personalities around the world." Other stories refer to a rescue worker from Zaka (an ultra-orthodox Rescue Service) who mentioned "dozens of beheaded babies". Another Zaka activist said he saw "a pregnant woman, her stomach was butchered".

"This story was false," continues the article, which then gives a detailed account of the known cases of dead children: A 10-month-old baby who was killed with his father in kibbutz Be'eri and a heavily pregnant Bedouin woman and her baby were killed by a rocket near Beer Sheva.

> *According to the National Insurance Institute, five other children aged 6 or under were murdered, including Omer Kedem Siman Tov, 2, and his 6-year-old twin sisters Arbel and Shachar, who were killed on Kibbutz Nir Oz. There was also 5-year-old Yazan Zakaria Abu Jama from Arara in the southern Negev, who was killed in a Hamas rocket strike, and 5-year-old Eitan Kapshetar, who was murdered with his parents and his 8-year-old sister, Aline, near Sderot. Fourteen children aged 12 to 15 were killed in Israel in rocket strikes launched from Gaza, not at massacre sites in southern Israeli communities. Most of the other children who were murdered were killed in or near their homes, usually with other family members.[26]*
>
> *There is no evidence that children from different families were killed together, which contradicts Netanyahu's claim to President Joe Biden that Hamas terrorists 'took dozens of children, tied them up, burned them and executed them.' [...]*
>
> *The IDF Spokesperson's Unit does not deny that Lt. Col. Buskila's remarks about babies strung up on clotheslines do not jibe with reality. It said: 'The officer serves as a reservist operations officer. He arrived at a large number of scenes after the attack and saw many difficult sights as part of his duties. The details of the incident will be clarified with the officer, and it will be made clear to him that he should not describe events whose details are unclear and unofficial'.*
>
> *As for Col. Vach's remarks on the bodies of eight burned babies, the IDF Spokesperson's Unit said he 'described difficult sights that he saw during his various missions evacuating bodies at the start of the war. The review was conducted in English, and the officer used the word 'babies' to describe a number of children's bodies that were found. The error was made in good faith and does not mitigate the severity of the atrocities committed.'*

Some of the incorrect descriptions were made by Zaka personnel; one repeatedly talked about 20 bound and burned bodies of children at a kibbutz. He told Haaretz that these were boys and girls between 10 and 15 found behind Kibbutz Kfar Azza's dining hall. Elsewhere, he said he saw 20 children from Kibbutz Be'eri laid next to each other and burned to death with their hands bound.

This description does not conform to the list of the dead. The teenagers murdered on Kfar Azza were Yiftach Kutz, 14, and his brother, Yonatan, 16. Their sister, Rotem, an 18-year-old soldier, was murdered with them. Nine minors were murdered at Be'eri; at least some of them were with their parents and killed in their homes, so it is possible that 20 bodies were all in one place.

Israeli army spokespersons claim that it was so messy that it was difficult to see what had happened. Zaka argues that their volunteers do not have the medical knowledge to say what happened and claim that the stories were told in good faith. A common feature of the allegations is to excuse the lack of evidence with the confusion that reigned.

Despite denials and clarifications, more than two months after October 7, on December 12, 2023, Biden said during an activity in Washington for the 2024 election campaign:

I saw some of the photographs when I was there — tying a mother and her daughter together on a rope and then pouring kerosene on them and then burning them, beheading infants, doing things that are just inhuman — totally, completely inhuman.[27]

The IDF spokesman told *The Intercept*:[28]

When we were there… we couldn't see it with our own eyes, but of course it happened. We can't confirm it officially from the army, but you've seen, I guess, videos on social media, you've seen girls with blood on their buttocks, it's a given that this has happened. Specifically on decapitated babies, we can't confirm how many there were or where it was.

Similarly, regarding the absence of medical evidence of rape and other sexual abuse, it was argued that:

here have been so many horrible situations and we don't have time, and we're currently busy fighting and defending our country. We don't have the time to check every report.

Yaniv Kubovioch wrote under the headline *"Graphic Videos and Incitement: How the IDF Misleads Israelis on Telegram"* in the Israeli *Haaretz* on December 12, 2023:[29]

> *The IDF unit responsible for psychological warfare operations operates a Telegram channel called 72 Virgins – Uncensored, which targets local audiences with 'exclusive content from the Gaza Strip' ... The channel was created as The Avengers on October 9, two days after the war began. The next day the name was changed to Azazel, echoing the Hebrew pronunciation of 'Gaza' and a word for hell, and then 72 Virgins – Uncensored. An October 11 post read: 'Burning their mother ... You won't believe the video we got! You can hear the crunch of their bones. We'll upload it right away, get ready.' Images of Palestinian captives and the bodies of terrorists were captioned 'Exterminating the roaches... exterminating the Hamas rats... Share this beauty.' The following text accompanies a video of an Israeli soldier allegedly dipping machine gun bullets in pork fat: 'What a man!!!!! Lubricates bullets with lard. You won't get your virgins.' And: 'Garbage juice!!!! Another dead terrorist!! You have to watch it with the sound, you'll die laughing.'*

The IDF denied first any involvement, but Yaniv Kubovich wrote in Haaretz[30] that "Maj. Gen. Oded Basyuk, head of the Operations Directorate, found that the information that led to the original denial that the channel was operated by or on behalf of the army was incorrect, and relied on misinformation relayed by members of the Influencing Department. In the wake of these findings, the unit's wartime commander is to end his military service."

The site "didn't stop at images from Gaza. On October 11, hundreds of Israelis, including members of the Beitar Jerusalem soccer team's violently racist fan club La Familia, rioted at Sheba Medical Center, Tel Hashomer, near Tel Aviv, following a rumour that Hamas terrorists who had invaded Israel were being treated there. People roamed the hospital, cursing out and spitting on medical professionals. Within an hour, a video of the riot was posted to the 72 Virgins channel with the title, "My brothers, the heroesssss, La Familia fans, love you!!!!!!! What heroes, they came to screw the Arabs."

Why did so many people die on October 7?

This is not a mathematical exercise. Every dead person is a tragedy, whether a Jew, a Palestinian, foreign worker, or tourist. Soldier or civilian. Young or old, male or female. Every life violently extinguished is a grieving family and friends, dreams and hopes dashed, opportunities never realized. One of the fundamental principles of the Geneva Conventions[31] (the laws of war) is to distinguish between *combatants* and *non-combatants* (who are called *"protected persons"*): *the principle of distinction.* Civilians, and all medical personnel, wounded and injured soldiers, soldiers who have laid down their arms, prisoners of war, aid workers, and the civilian population in occupied territories, i.e., all those who are not or who "are no longer enemies but merely suffering people and defenceless human beings".[32] All permanent and temporary medical facilities are also protected and must not be attacked.

This is probably why the word "civilians" is emphasized when talking about victims. And preferably women and children, which targets our emotions. (As horrible as it is and as trivial as it may sound, killing enemy soldiers in war is legitimate under the laws of war).

In recent decades, we have learned that the term *collateral damage* refers to civilians killed in armed conflicts. The drafters of the conventions knew it is inevitable that civilians are harmed during armed conflict as a consequence of attacks on military, and therefore legitimate, targets. This is where the second principle comes in, the *principle of proportionality.* The harm caused to protected persons ("bystanders"), must be proportionate to the military advantage or benefit that the attack on the military target is expected to yield.

A first observation about October 7 is that there is only talk of Israeli casualties. How many militiamen from Hamas, Islamic Jihad, or other armed groups died is of no interest to the Western media. Nor the civilian Gazans who poured out of Gaza through the breaches in the barrier and were killed or wounded. We do not know how many there were, how many were armed and used their weapons to kill and wound other people, or how many, armed or not, took hostages into Gaza. It is quite possible and highly likely that some Gazans went through the breaches in the barrier out of curiosity, filled with joy at the sudden collapse of their prison walls. Some may have hoped to see the village from which their grandparents were driven in 1948, or simply wanted to see what the other side looked like. The population of Gaza is very young, and a large proportion of them are refugees and descendants of the refugees expelled by Jewish militias in 1948 or by the IDF in 1967. Perhaps we will never know how many ordinary Gazan civilians crossed the border and died and how many managed to come back unharmed. Figures mentioned are 3,000 dead – 1,500 of them Hamas men – but all this is very uncertain.

In this book, we also do not address the number of deaths during the bombings in Gaza after the October 7. We limit ourselves to the Israelis killed on October 7 or the days after, in Israel. The figures were slow in coming, with the first reasonably accurate lists published in early December 2023. While there is still uncertainty, the newspaper *Haaretz* has a list of names and other data that are continuously updated with figures of soldiers killed in the fighting,[33] but there are some difficulties with the figures. This list includes not only the people who died as a direct result of the attack on October 7 and the following days, but also all those who died after that date, in events related to the conflict. The list could easily be interpreted as an acknowledgement of how many people were killed, directly or indirectly, by the Hamas attack on October 7, but this is not the case. The list also includes the three Israeli hostages killed by the IDF on December 15 in Gaza, the Israeli hostages killed in Israel's bombings, the man killed by the IDF in Jerusalem on November 30, two killed in traffic accidents, three people killed in an attack in Egypt, several soldiers killed on the border with Lebanon and elsewhere in Israel, and all soldiers killed in combat in Gaza, including those killed by friendly fire, that is, killed accidentally by their comrades or by Israeli aerial bombing. Not all the dead are Jews. A number were Palestinian citizens of Israel (in Israel they are commonly called Israeli Arabs). Most of them were killed by rockets or other incidents in the cities – the kibbutzim or communities in the Gaza Envelope only admit Jews as residents and members, but it may be that Palestinian workers were in the kibbutzim and were also killed.

On January 5, 2024, *Haaretz's* list included 1,384 names. Of these, 827 are civilians, 59 police officers, 485 soldiers, and 13 emergency services personnel (among them 5 firefighters, 4 paramedics, 2 *Shin Bet* [Israel's security service]). Of the soldiers, 205 were killed in the fighting in Gaza after October 7, including those killed by friendly fire. We do not know how many of the hostages were killed as a result of Israeli bombing.

Age distribution; list published by *Haaretz:*

Under 10 years old	7
10 – 17	27
18 – 24	487
25 – 29	160
30 – 39	170
40 – 49	84
50 – 59	58
60 – 69	45
70 or older	47
Unknown	299
Total	1 384

The large number of 18- to 40-year-olds is explained by the fact that most of the soldiers are young people doing military service, and also by the large number of young partygoers killed at the Nova music festival.

Some articles mention 71 foreigners. Many Israelis have dual nationality; that is not what is meant here, but occasional tourists and foreign workers – 38 of them from Thailand, 3 from China, 3 from the Philippines, 2 from Sri Lanka and 1 from Moldova – and 10 students from Nepal. It may seem odd that Israel is "importing" cheap workers from so far away when it has a virtually unlimited number of Palestinians who will work for low wages. But it has been a stated Israeli policy for at least a couple of decades to replace Palestinian workers from the occupied territories with Thais and others, possibly not as cheap. In fact, this is not a recent policy. Already at the beginning of the establishment of the *Yishuv*, the Jewish colonies in Palestine, one hundred years ago, the Zionist policy was to use only Jewish labour – it was called "Conquest of labour" and consisted of "monopolizing all manual work, later all skilled work for Jewish workers".[34] The central trade union *Histadrut* (originally called the General Federation of Hebrew Workers in Eretz Israel) was created in the early 20th century to organize Jewish workers exclusively and was only opened to non-Jews in 1959.

* * *

It is remarkable that both the media and political leaders speak of "1,400 (or later 1,200) civilian victims of Hamas terror" ignoring the significant proportion of soldiers among the dead. Another surprising thing is the lack of information about the wounded and interviews with them. *Haaretz* tried unsuccessfully to get this information from the military for almost two months.[35] In early December, the IDF published a figure for the number of wounded soldiers: 1,593 since the beginning of the war – which seems to be a very low figure. *Haaretz* has obtained data from some hospitals that point to a much higher number of wounded soldiers. The Ministry of Health has reported 10,548 wounded in total.

The IDF's figures seem remarkably low because one would expect a large proportion of the wounded to be soldiers. Another undisclosed figure is for non-military wounded, such as rescue workers, police officers, border guards, *Shin Bet* security services, ambulance staff, and others from Magen David Adom (the Israeli equivalent of the Red Cross).

According to the newspaper, the military has demanded that hospitals get permission from the IDF's information department before publishing data related to the war. Hospital staff have reacted strongly against this requirement because they consider their work part of the national effort and are keen to show what they do and achieve.

"It would not be morally sound to investigate..."

Israelis may have been killed by Hamas or other Palestinian militiamen, by Gazan civilians who escaped through the many breaches (up to 30 or more breaches were created in the "security barrier" surrounding Gaza); others may have been killed in crossfire in the fighting that broke out between militiamen and Israeli military, police, or security guards in various locations; and still others died by what is known as friendly fire – killed by their own side.

An example of friendly fire is the case of Yuval Kestelman, who was mistakenly killed by soldiers in Jerusalem on November 30[36] while intervening against a terrorist attack. According to the family, it was a straightforward execution. Even more notable are the three Israelis who managed to escape from their guards in Gaza on December 15 but were killed by Israeli soldiers.[37]

Yedioth Ahronoth is one of the largest daily newspapers in Israel and *Ynet* is its internet site. On December 12, 2023, Yoav Zitun wrote in *Ynet* under the title "*One-fifth of troop fatalities in Gaza due to friendly fire or accidents*" (20 out of 105).[38] This is not unusual in an armed conflict where accidents happen, and mistakes are made. The article also states that this number

> *is minimal and doesn't refer to the first three weeks preceding the ground escalation, regarding the casualties on October 7, nor does it include other fronts. For example, an IDF officer was killed as a result of a friendly fire incident near Qalqilya at the beginning of the war, and other soldiers were killed as a result of a tank overturning near the Lebanon border...At least one was killed by an Israeli airstrike when an attack helicopter fired on a building where soldiers were located last week.*

Yoav Zitun further writes:

> *Casualties fell as a result of friendly fire on October 7, but the IDF believes that beyond the operational investigations of the events, it would not be morally sound to investigate these incidents due to the immense and complex quantity of them that took place in the kibbutzim and southern Israeli communities due to the challenging situations the soldiers were in at the time.*

The last paragraph is remarkable to say the least and leads to several conclusions:

- The number of deaths from friendly fire on October 7 was extensive ("the immense and complex quantity of them that took place in the kibbutzim and southern Israeli communities").

- The soldiers didn't always know what they were doing ("challenging situations the soldiers were in at the time").

- It seems to communicate fears of the consequences of public opinion in Israel and probably also abroad if the truth comes out, which is probably why the IDF believes that "it would not be morally sound to investigate" these events.

Several reports point to the same problem. In *Haaretz*, Amos Harel writes:[39]

The Coordination and Liaison Office was attacked on October 7 together with all the outposts along the division's line. A large Hamas force seized the adjacent Erez Crossing, which was closed for the Simhat Torah holiday. From there, within minutes and with no resistance, they advanced into the military base, killing and kidnapping the soldiers of the Civil Administration,[40] though a few of them managed to return fire before being hit… Brig. Gen. Rosenfeld entrenched himself in the division's subterranean war room together with a handful of male and female soldiers, trying desperately to rescue and organize the sector under attack. Many of the soldiers, most of them not combat personnel, were killed or wounded outside. The division was compelled to request an aerial strike against the base itself in order to repulse the terrorists.

In plain language: the general asked for his base to be bombed.

The Israeli government's spokesperson for foreign media, Mark Regev, announced on November 10, 2023, that the death toll tally had been revised down from 1,400 to 1,200.[41] His explanation was that "we made a mistake, there were actually bodies that were so badly burnt we thought they were ours; in the end apparently they were Hamas terrorists".

He seemed to be referring to the same thing that Brigadier General Eyal Karin, the IDF Chief Rabbi, had said just a few days after the attack, the October 13,[42] when he said that,

"a considerable number of the fallen soldiers are not easily identifiable and their identification requires the use of advanced technology. This process

How does this relate?

Hamas militiamen had hardly burned themselves or each other. It is very difficult to understand how they would have taken the time to burn people. How much gasoline, explosives, and/or time is required to burn human bodies to the point where identification becomes such a complicated process?

And did Hamas carry such weapons in para-gliders, on motorcycles, and in cars that they used when entering Israel?

Was there was no evidence to make it possible to certify whether they were Hamas militiamen or Israeli civilians: clothes, weapons, the position of the bodies, the place where they were found?

The IDF published a short, shocking video of a burnt-out car in which some bodies are completely charred.[43] Only black remains of the skeletons are visible and the metal carcass of the car. The only reasonable explanation is that these people were burned so badly by a very powerful blast caused by a rocket or shell fired from powerful artillery or a missile from a helicopter or airplane. So, by the IDF. (Hamas do not have access to this kind of weapons.)

But then another question arises: does Israel believe that it could have killed its own citizens? Is this what lies behind the mysterious claim by Yoav Zitun in *Ynet* on December 12, that "the immense and complex quantity" made it not "morally sound to investigate"?

When one looks at the reports, videos, and photographs from the major media, it is astounding to behold the enormous destruction presented. Large numbers of cars and houses completely demolished and large areas of burnt land, especially in the festival area. (This contrasts, incidentally, with the poor editing of many presentations by major media groups and TV channels, especially from the US, where the images shown are not consistent with what the speaker is saying. I lost count of the number of times I rewound the video clips to see whether the car had any bullet holes, whether there were blood stains on the roads or the walls, to look for the shell casings mentioned – perhaps it was done out of an exaggerated respect for sensitive viewers, but it is nonetheless surprising.) Destroyed houses could to some extent be the result of Hamas rockets, but the explanation given was always that it was Hamas militiamen who had destroyed the houses on the spot and then burned them in what was considered proof of Hamas's brutality and eagerness to destroy, as if driven by a demonic, uncontrollable rage. Why? Were they so bestial? And if so, how did they manage to do it? The same questions about the burnt bodies arise here: did they carry such heavy weapons in para-gliders to demolish so many houses and cars? What large amounts of ammunition and fuel must have been needed to cause such massive destruction?

"They killed everyone, including the hostages"

An *ABC News* article begins with a seven-minute video by David Muir entitled "Israel's Ground Zero".[44] (Many people are saying that October 7 was Israel's 9-11. There is at least one feature in common: it is the first time that the war can be said to really have moved into Israel's own territory).

The video begins with two militiamen approaching the gate of a kibbutz. One of them tries to crawl under the gate but fails and proceeds to the guardhouse, breaks the window, and enters. The narrator says,

> *As the video continued, the two gunmen were seen rushing through the now open gate, one ripping down the surveillance camera as he ran into the sleepy enclave. But other cameras stationed nearby recorded the militants headed into the community to join other Hamas fighters who entered from four or five directions as they went about hunting down victims, military officials said... The video, posted online, recorded a car pulling up at about 6:30 a.m. and pausing until the automatic gate began to slide open. A second terrorist was seen emerging from the shadows beside the gate and opening fire with an assault-type weapon on the unsuspecting occupants of the vehicle, killing them. Their car was later found still parked at the entrance gate, torched.*

Muir speaks in the film: "The video shows Hamas militia taking hostages in the street, hands behind their backs, you see people walking in the street. Then you see people lying motionless in the street. They are dead." One can see some people being forced to walk in the street. The camera focuses on something in the street, a few metres away, but the image is masked, and it is impossible to see what it is.

Muir speaks to the camera and approaches the gate of the kibbutz ... "We see the broken window of the guard shack and the burnt car standing at the gate". (This is an irrelevant detail, but it is not the same car. The shape of the rear window is different, and the burnt car has a spoiler extending the roof which is missing from the Mazda seen on the CCTV camera as it drove up to the gate.)

The video shows several demolished houses, and two military officers are interviewed, Major General Itai Veruv and Major Libby Weiss. "In this house, fourteen people were held hostage for hours of terror... a massacre, 112 residents of this community were killed, people were murdered, you can see the destruction… they came at six in the morning and slaughtered them in their beds."

"There are no words," says Major General Veruv. "It's something between ISIS and Pogam…" [he means pogrom] "…residents of Be'eri were killed by knife, by hand grenades, by fire," says Veruv. "Children were killed in front of their mothers, and mothers in front of their children. People were killed with their hands tied…"

Brigadier General Barak Hiram was interviewed on October 26 by Ilana Dayan, host of *Uvda* on the Israeli *Channel 12*.[45] He said that at a certain point "Nissim Hazan, who was the commander of a tank, came with the first tank to the kibbutz, and I gave permission to fire at the house to stop the terrorists".

The video shows a tank firing into a built-up area, then a TV clip from that day showing from the air at least five or six houses with their roofs gone.

The journalist says: "there were no kidnapped people in the houses". The general does not respond directly but says that one of the hostages managed to escape and a situation arose that suggested the terrorists wanted to negotiate, but that the terrorists responded with an RPG and that he then ordered a force to storm the house and rescue the hostages. He believes that there may have been twenty hostages and that they managed to rescue four and the others were killed in cold blood by the militants. They counted 26 bodies of terrorists, he says, adding that "…we found eight children tied together and shot, a couple, man and woman, tied together and shot…".

These statements, disseminated in the media worldwide, were made by spokespersons of the Israeli army, but there are other versions. Yasmin Porat lives in northern Israel and was at the Nova music festival with her husband, Tal Katz and survived the massacre in kibbutz Be'eri. On October 15, 2023, Porat was interviewed by journalist Aryeh Golan on the program *Haboker Hazeh* on the Israeli public radio *Kan*. *Electronic Intifada* published an article about this as soon after this, on October 16. It was updated a week later with new information and a translation of the full interview in English (the original article was retained).[46]

In the interview, Porat says that when the attack started, she fled with her husband to the community of Be'eri and was allowed to enter the house of Adi and Hadas Dagan, an elderly couple. Hamas men came to the house, and took them to Pessi Cohen's house, where there were already eight hostages and up to forty Hamas men guarding them. The journalist asks if they were mistreated, and she replies, "they treated us very humanely… They wanted to take us as hostages to Gaza, not kill us". They were given water and calmed down by the kidnappers and allowed to go out on the lawn to escape the heat inside. Porat says the kidnappers had taken a Palestinian bus driver from Jerusalem, Suhayb al-Razim, and forced him to translate into Hebrew. The Hamas leader, a man in his 30s, later identified as Hasan Hamduna, wanted Porat to call the police. The kidnappers believed that the Israeli army was in control of the area and wanted to negotiate free passage back to Gaza – the hostages would be released at the border. Porat called the police several times and was asked to exaggerate the number of hostages to 40. The Hamas leader was allowed to speak to an Israeli officer who spoke Arabic and after their brief conversation they waited for the security forces, but when the military arrived all hell broke loose. The shooting was intense. She describes how five or six hostages were shot, not by the Hamas men but in the crossfire. The journalist asks: "Crossfire, so it could also be from our forces?" She answers "Undoubtedly". Hasan Hamduna decided to surrender and had to come out, naked (to make sure he had no weapons), with Porat. When she got to the soldiers, she asked them to stop shooting, which they did at first. She saw some of the hostages lying on the grass; they all eventually died. Porat said:

> *"They eliminated everyone, including the hostages. Because there was very, very heavy crossfire. I was freed at approximately 5:30. The fighting apparently ended at 8:30. After an insane crossfire, two tank shells were shot into the house. It's a small kibbutz house, nothing big. You saw it on the news.*

Among the dead were Adi Dagan and Porat's partner, Tal Katz. Hadas Dagan was wounded but survived. On December 9, she appeared for the first time on *Channel 12, TV3*.[47] Dagan's story (translated by David Sheen of *Electronic Intifada*)[48] confirms the central elements of Porat's testimony:

> 'It's obvious that this incident presents a very heavy moral dilemma. I don't want someone to take the story with the very difficult moral dilemma presented here and point an accusatory finger at the army,' Dagan says when identifying the immediate cause of her husband's death. 'To me it's very clear that me and Adi were wounded from the shrapnel from the tank shell because it happened at that very moment'.

She describes the horror of watching her husband bleed from a hole in his neck next to her, until he stopped moving. Hadas Dagan and Yasmin Porat were the only survivors from that house.

It was not Hamas men who interrupted the negotiations and started firing, as General Hiram claimed in the interview, and no attempt was made to rescue the hostages.

On October 20, *Haaretz*, in its Hebrew edition, published an interview with a man named Tuval who lived on Kibbutz Be'eri, but was away on October 7. Tuval's partner was killed that day. The newspaper reports:

According to him [Tuval], only on Monday night and only after the commanders in the field made difficult decisions – including shelling houses with all their occupants inside in order to eliminate the terrorists along with the hostages – did the IDF complete the takeover of the kibbutz. The price was terrible: at least 112 Be'eri people were killed. Others were kidnapped. Yesterday, 11 days after the massacre, the bodies of a mother and her son were discovered in one of the destroyed houses. It is believed that more bodies are still lying in the rubble.[49]

In the British newspaper, *The Guardian*, Quique Kierszenbaum reported[50] on October 11 on her trip to Kibbutz Be'eri, organized by the Israeli army's propaganda unit:

Building after building has been destroyed, whether in the Hamas assault or in the fighting that followed, nearby trees splintered, and walls reduced to concrete rubble from where Israeli tanks blasted the Hamas militants where they were hiding. Floors collapsed on floors. Roof beams were tangled and exposed like rib cages.

On December 15, military veteran Erez Tidhar shared his experiences from Kibbutz Be'eri:[51]

Every minute a missile comes down on you, every minute. And suddenly you see a missile from a helicopter that fires into the kibbutz. You say to yourself, I don't get it – an IDF helicopter firing into an Israeli kibbutz. And you see a tank driving through the streets of the kibbutz flanking the cannon and firing a shell into a house. There are things that you cannot comprehend. And then I suddenly see on the right side, hundreds of people from the kibbutz...

Idan Kazas, from the Eitam Rescue and Evacuation Unit, said:

"And people with children in their arms, without shoes, people that escaped, fleeing, like refugees. My feeling was that I had reached – like an American soldier that arrived on April 14, 1945, at Bergen Belsen – like, some kind of refugees.

Erez Tidhar again:

"At some point, very quickly we said, wait a minute, someone has to get these folks out of here because it doesn't make sense. Because missiles are flying around and shooting is going on. A war zone. In the end, they got out of that hell inside the kibbutz and then what, they will get hit by a missile at the entrance of the kibbutz. Because of what? Wait for who? So, we placed all the unit's vehicles and we started loading the people and drove them somewhere out of the fighting zone.

On December 19, *Channel 12* published a video from a helicopter where the audio was translated into English and published on December 24, 2023, by *Electronic Intifada*.[52] The video has been edited. A female voice says:

For the first time since October 7, we get a rare opportunity to see the tragedy of Kibbutz Be'eri from above, as the fighters and the population saw in real time. At 4:20 pm, more than nine hours after hundreds of terrorists broke into Be'eri, whole neighborhoods of the kibbutz up in flames.

We see the kibbutz from the helicopter, then from inside a house you see a tank approaching and aiming at the camera. Yasmin Porat appears and says,

"there is a tank coming and I asked one of the soldiers: But if you shoot shells, won't they harm the hostages? He tells me 'No, we're only doing it on the sides, to take down walls'."

The speaker voice says:

This raises more questions about the IDF's and YAMAM's actions. Hagas Dagan tells us about the shrapnel from an Israeli shell that injured her and killed her husband. The tank is seen firing at the Pessis house at around 17:30, an hour and a half after the troops arrived.

The voice continues as a large number of vehicles are seen at an intersection:

The next clip highlights an additional failure. Many forces waited at the entrance to Be'eri in the afternoon and didn't enter. This convoy of vehicles was seen already on Saturday at 4:30 PM at the height of the battle inside. One man says that at 18:10 he saw 'a force of hundreds of soldiers, dozens of vehicles from the Border Police and others. The soldiers were armoured from head to toe... I personally approached every officer, including a major: 'Who is in charge here? Who is the commander?' [All] replied: 'No, I'm only in charge of these five'... 'But who's in charge of everything, who is in command overall?' No one knew. The command appeared to be in total chaos. And I tell them: 'Guys, inside they're fighting and slaughtering families, we have to enter'. And no one listened to me.

Then a woman appears and says:

> *When we emerged, I went soldier to a soldier and yelled: 'Who is returning to Be'eri? And I went right up to them: 'It can't be that you're standing here. People are screaming for help on the kibbutz. [But] everyone just stands there. No one speaks, no one says, 'Me'.*

Another very upset man tells more or less the same story:

> *Five hundred soldiers standing outside, organized, with dogs, with weaponry, with protection, with vehicles, standing outside and no one organized them. [We] run inside and pull children out of the burning reinforced safety rooms! And mothers, elderly people! Every minute, people here [they] lost blood. And the army... [did] nothing. It was here standing outside; it didn't understand what was going on here.*

The female narrator says:

> *These days the IDF is busy battling in the Gaza Strip and the important investigations into the failures of October 7 have yet to begin. The video we exposed here sheds light on the Black Sabbath but two months later, the residents of Be'eri and other Gaza envelope residents in cities, moshavim, and kibbutzim deserve to receive answers. There was a command problem and the courage to fight and attack simply wasn't there.*

A male voice says:

> *These were hours when we needed to fill the kibbutz with soldiers. Many questions must be asked. The response of the IDF spokesperson: 'We will carry out a deep detailed investigation to clarify all the details when the situation allows it, and we will make the evidence public.'*

Former Israeli Prime Minister Neftali Bennet wrote on X (Twitter) on November 14:[53]

> *12-year-old Liel Hetzroni of Kibbutz Beeri was murdered in her home by Hamas monsters on Oct 7th. Her body has now been identified. Her brother and grandfather were also murdered. Look at her sweet smile. Liel harmed nobody. She was murdered just because she's Jewish. We're fighting the most just war: to ensure this can never happen again. Nobody should ask us to stop, nor will we, before we achieve that goal.*

For him, this girl's death is an argument for continuing the war. But the two who were there and survived, Yasmin Porat and Hadas Dagan, have a different version of what happened. Porat told state radio station *Kan*[54] on November 15 about conversations she had with Dagan about the girl Liel Hetzroni: "She did not stop screaming", Porat remembers Dagan telling her. "Yasmin, when those two shells hit, she stopped screaming. There was silence then." Porat's conclusion is that she was incinerated by the tank shell and therefore could not be identified until one month later.

In a YouTube clip aired by the *i24NEWS*, some female Israeli soldiers on a tank were proud to serve in the first all-female tank in the world.[55] The girls tell about the firing during hours and then were ordered by the commanding officer to shoot at everyone:

> *No matter what comes from that route, you open fire; you have permission; if in doubt, of course, check, but no matter what comes from the North to the South you fire … They drove in to the settlement and] a soldier ran towards me – like such a blur – running to me in a panic, he raised his hands and shouted: Terrorists! Terrorists have entered the kibbutz … I asked: there are civilians there? I don't know, fire a shell … I fired machine guns into the entrance of the house. The tank fired both machine guns and shells even within the community. Basically, a very complex fight … the terrorists didn't attack the tank, they fled or died … the battle lasted until 20:00.*

What is expressed in this section can be perceived as shocking. Could Israel really have killed a significant proportion of those who died on October 7? One of those who argue this is Chas W. Freeman, a former US diplomat, in an interview with Thomas Karat that was circulated on X and reproduced in the *Jewish Voice for Labor*.[56] Freeman argues that the IDF acted in a chaotic manner and that most of those killed at the Nova music festival fell victim to Hellfire missiles fired from helicopters.

Among the many points he makes are these (H/t Arnaud Bertrand and for the transcript below)

- *Israel's response on October 7 was a "disgrace in military terms" taking a terrible toll on Israelis;*

- *Hamas was successful in putting the Palestinian self-determination issue back on the global agenda and in bolstering support among Palestinians for its willingness to resist;*

- *Israel will not recover its image as a historical refuge for victims of oppression but will be remembered as the home of perpetrators of genocide. […]*

Key points in the video:
— He agrees that many of the victims of Oct 7th were killed by the Israeli army in the form of "undisciplined fire by helicopters with hellfire missiles or by tanks with incendiary rounds directed at buildings". In the case of the victims of the music festival he even says they "were largely killed, it appears, by hellfire missiles and by other undisciplined fire by Israeli forces". To him this "disgrace in military terms" stems from a "lack of discipline and training necessary to respond" but also from the IDF's "Hannibal directive", which "says that rather than get into bargaining over hostage exchange you should just kill the Israeli hostages along with their captors."

Al Jazeera released a video on 10 March 2024 entitled "Al Jazeera investigation finds Israeli military likely involved in October 7 'friendly fire' deaths".[57]

"In the chaotic early hours of October 7 Israeli forces scrambled to engage Hamas Fighters with Apache helicopter gunships which fired onto cars driving towards Gaza aware that some of them were carrying captives".

The 8-minute video is a harrowing experience with embedded video showing the firing on cars and people without knowing who they are. "This is an outrage, I mean, what kind of way is this to fight a modern war?" says Professor Chuck Frielich, security advisor to the Israeli government from 2000-2005, while Chris Cobb-Smith, security analyst, says it is "inexcusable for a helicopter or any weapon system to be engaging any target if you don't know what that target is. Now my concern is with this footage we cannot tell whether there Hamas gunmen or civilians or possibly hostages and I don't believe the helicopter pilot or the machine gun operator would be able to tell either." Andreas Krieg, a security analyst at King's College London, says "These big rounds have a certain area effect and obviously come at a certain rate that if you shoot at a group of people, you're most likely going to kill everyone you are knowingly putting your own civilians at risk."

"The investigative unit asked the Israeli Army for comment on its actions on October 7. They did not reply", says Peter Charlie, Al Jazeera.

The last guest is Justin Schlosberg, co-founder of the Institute for Journalism and Social Change from London. He explains that he believes it is likely that Hamas committed horrific atrocities and war crimes and he thinks the majority of the dead fell to Hamas, but that "friendly fire incidents" occurred as a result of the way Israel ran the war from day one. However, his key message is that the most important thing is to expose how the Israeli government and some people in the media *created a narrative to justify what amounts in my view to a genocide in Gaza. I think it's really important to look at how these stories were amplified by mainstream media across the globe and how little care was taken by so many journalists to really ascertain the degree to which these stories were true. Obviously, there are the stories that were thoroughly debunked as the deliberate massacre of babies. The first casualty of war is truth and people rely on journalists. Journalists' task is to cut through the fog as far as possible and if they can't at least be honest about what we don't know. Too many journalists took things that were coming from the Israeli government and from right-wing commentators as facts when they never should have been.*

"There is a growing awareness in Israel now that this war is being fought on false pretences in the sense that clearly there is no way in which what the government says it aims to achieve from the war – any sense of security or long-term peace for the Israeli people without changing the policy of occupation and oppression of the Palestinians. I think that this is leading to very serious questions about how Israel is prosecuting this war from day one …the very grave mistakes and probably in some cases deliberate misjudgements on the part of the IDF and the Israeli government which has put hostages at risk."

Two weeks after the October 7 attack, an author from Israel who wishes to remain anonymous wrote in *Mondoweiss:*[58]

It brings back to my mind the events of August 1, 2014, during the most violent Israeli campaign against Gaza up to the current one. On August 1, there was a ceasefire, but an Israeli unit initiated a provocation that ended with the capture of one of its soldiers by Palestinian militants. The Israeli response was devastating, clearly designed to make sure that the soldier, Hadar Goldin, would be dead with as many Palestinians as possible. According to investigations by Amnesty International and the United Nations[59] 'the massive Israeli bombardment killed between 135 and 200 Palestinian civilians, including 75 children, in the three hours following the suspected capture of the one Israeli soldier.'

These events are not accidental local eruptions of the 'Samsonian' desire to die (or let your soldiers die) with one's enemies. It is a well-documented official policy of the Israeli army, at least since 1986, known as the 'Hannibal Directive', the 'Hannibal code', or the 'Hannibal doctrine'.

The Hannibal Directive

The Hannibal Doctrine or Directive was formulated in the summer of 1986 in Lebanon after Israel agreed to a prisoner exchange (the *Jibril Agreement*) in which 1,150 Palestinian prisoners were released in exchange for the release of three captured Israeli soldiers. The directive, named after a Carthaginian general who took his life to avoid falling into enemy hands, is to prevent the capture of a soldier by all means, even at the risk of harming him.[60]

When the case related in the previous page in 2014 the IDF was at war, unlike the situation in 2006, when Gilad Shalit was captured by Hamas (he was exchanged five years later for 1,027 Palestinian prisoners). In 2014, the army leadership did not have to say much to explain what was to be done. One word was enough: *Hannibal.*

In Israel, which, according to a Knesset member, is "democratic towards Jews, and Jewish towards Arabs",[61] there is a functioning judiciary system. (For the time being: the government wants to change the rules for appointing judges, which has caused major protests, not least among reservists). Lawyers,[62] judges, and the Association of Civil Rights in Israel[63] condemned the Hannibal Directive as illegal, a violation of the principle of distinction between civilians and military in war and a method of warfare that violates international law. Commander-in-Chief Gadi Eizenkot abolished the directive in 2016, but this seems to have had little effect. A growing number of reports gave clear indications that the Hannibal Directive was applied on October 7.

On November 11, 2023,[64] *Electronic Intifada* cites an article by Yoav Zitun in *Ynet*[65] published as early as October 15, in Hebrew only, with an embedded video shot from inside a helicopter shooting at cars and people walking or running. Fifteen seconds into the video, one person can be seen pushing another in front of him – one can guess it is a Hamas militiaman with a captured Israeli hostage being taken to Gaza. The next second, the pilot shoots them both.

> *The first helicopters were summoned from the north ironically, and reached the Gaza envelope about an hour after the battles began... The pilots fired at those who crossed the fence, and even right inside the settlements. The pilots received information from the ground to their mobile phones. In four hours, 300 targets were attacked, most in Israeli territory. [...]*
>
> *After the pilots realized that inside the army stations and the settlements that were conquered, it was very difficult to distinguish between terrorists and [Israeli] soldiers or civilians, the decision was made that the first*

objective of the fighter helicopters and the armed Zik [Elbit Hermes 450] drones was to stop the deluge of terrorists and the murderous masses that flowed into Israeli territory through the holes in the fence. Twenty-eight fighter helicopters shot over the course of the day all of the ammunition in their bellies, in renewed runs to rearm. We are talking about hundreds of 30-millimetre cannon mortars (each mortar is like a hand grenade) and Hellfire missiles. The frequency of fire at the thousands of terrorists was enormous at the start, and only at a certain point did the pilots begin to slow their attacks and carefully choose the targets.

Hamas made it difficult for helicopter pilots and the drone operators: the investigation revealed that the invading forces were instructed in their final briefings to march slowly towards the settlements and army stations, and inside them, and not to run under any circumstances, to make the pilots think they were Israelis. The deception worked for a considerable while, until the Apache pilots understood they needed to sidestep their restrictions. Only around 9:00 did some start on their own initiative to spray the terror-ists with cannons, without permission from their superiors.

The air activity on the first day was not organized, and in the skies, pilots had to improvise solutions to the complicated and unprecedented situation: much of the firing and targeting directions received from forces battling on the ground reached the pilots via phone calls or images sent by WhatsApp. Reflecting on the enormous number of murdered and kidnapped, the Air Force is convinced that without the fire support and many attacks carried out by the IDF fighter helicopter pilots on that day, the carnage would have been much greater.

Zitun cites the startling case of one Lieutenant Colonel A., the commander of Squadron 190 who around mid-morning of October 7,

'instructed the other fighters in the air to shoot at everything they see in the area of the fence, and at a certain point also attacked an IDF [Israeli army] station with trapped soldiers in order to help the fighters of Navy Commando Unit 13 attack it and liberate it'.

One wonders what they were thinking. What could have led them to think that those who had planned the action would assume that Israelis would not run in such a situation? Or is it an afterthought to excuse themselves for killing so many people whom they couldn't identify?

Legacy Conversations is a *YouTube* site run by South African former military personnel. Under the heading "Legacy Special Report on Israel vs HAMAS", on November 14,[66] a retired Israeli major, Graeme Ipp, is interviewed by Koos Kotze, who claims that Israeli aircraft attacked vehicles in which Hamas was transporting prisoners to Gaza after raiding kibbutzim and barracks, killing both Hamas soldiers and hostages. (Graeme may be a fictitious name).

On November 19, a police source in *The Times of Israel*[67] reacts to "a claim in Haaretz that an IDF helicopter that arrived at the site of the Supernova festival near Re'im on October 7 may have killed some Israeli civilians".[68]

The Times of Israel reports on a statement from the police claiming that "the investigation focused only and solely on police activity, and not on any IDF activity, and therefore did not provide 'any indication about the harm of civilians due to aerial activity there." The police urged the press to "take responsibility for their publications and only base stories on official sources...". The journalist in *The Times of Israel* concludes that "elements of the Haaretz article were taken widely out of context on social media and *used to blame Israel for hundreds of civilian deaths on October 7*, none of which has any basis in fact and in extensive reporting about the massacre" (Emphasis added).

We probably should interpret this statement as an admission.

On December 5, Asa Winstanley wrote in *Electronic Intifada*: "We blew up Israeli houses on October 7, says a colonel."[69] His article includes several embedded videos and the translation of an interview in Hebrew in which journalist Lion Kodner interviews Colonel Nof Erez on *Haaretz's The Week* podcast.

The Palestinian military assault that morning was so successful that it became impossible to get authorization from senior officers. Dozens of army bases were commandeered by Hamas, which targeted communications throughout the region. The regional military leadership was quickly eliminated. Colonel Erez says:

> *The way a helicopter squadron works is it arrives at the area of activity and tries to speak to the division command. There was no division command at that stage. Even by 6:30 [am] there was no division command. If unsuccessful, it speaks with the brigade command. It too wasn't [responsive] by... then. And the battalion command, Battalion 13 that was there in the area, it too, unfortunately, was... not easily reachable. By the way, I know some stories of attack helicopter pilots that communicated via cellular phones with the settlement emergency squads, who coordinated with them firing inside the settlements by cellular phone.*

Kodner asks about "rumors that the army bombed all kinds of houses inside the settlements, the Hannibal Directive, and all kinds of conspiracy theories running around in the first few days". Colonel Erez hesitates, but admits that the air force did blow up houses, "but never without permission".

"The Hannibal Directive was apparently applied at a certain stage, because at that moment they understand there is a kidnapping, they immediately say, 'Guys, this is Hannibal.' But the Hannibal we trained for all of the last twenty years, is for a vehicle we know at what point of the fence it enters, on what side it drives, and maybe even on which road it drives. This was a mass Hannibal. There were tons and tons of openings in the fence, and thousands of people in every type of vehicle, some with hostages and some without. It was an impossible mission to identify and to do what they did. I know that whoever had weapons at hand, the attack helicopters and the drones, did everything they could – without control, without coordination with ground forces, because there were none in the first stage. Later on, when army forces had already arrived, there were a few more people to talk to. By the way, the special units arrived pretty quickly, but they didn't work as units, they worked as individuals, and that's also why we saw the numbers of wounded among MATKAL and SHALDAG commandos [special units of Israeli forces]. They didn't work connected..." (Emphasis added)

"Controversial procedures"

A month after Sagi Cohens wrote about "Conspiracy theories and lies – denial of the October 7 Hamas massacre is gaining ground online", Noa Limone wrote in the same newspaper[70] under the headline "If Israel has used a controversial procedure against its citizens, now is the time to talk about it". The article deals with the Hannibal Directive – she quotes Yasmin Porat and General Hiram about Kibbutz Be'eri – and the author wonders how to explain that no one in Israel reacts to the news that a tank fired at a house in a kibbutz where there were Hamas men but also hostages: Is it grief, fear that it only helps those who deny the Hamas massacre, or – she is very careful with language – the ethos?

According to the Cambridge dictionary *ethos* means: "the set of beliefs, ideas, etc., about the social behaviour and relationships of a person or group". In plain language: the moral values of the individual and society.

It is easy to understand that it must feel heavy to write that the Israeli society is morally numb. But that's what she writes about:

> *... the ethos prevailing in the Israeli military and society in recent years, which may have influenced the decision-making in the field and the public mood. Although the Hannibal Directive does not say that a soldier can be killed to prevent them from falling into enemy hands, many officers and soldiers in the field interpret it that way. To this must be added the IDF's increasingly loose open-fire regulations, the tragic consequences of which we saw in the killing by an off-duty soldier of Israeli civilian Yuval Doron Kestelman at the scene of a terror attack. The perceptions in the military and society feed each other symbiotically. Their consequences should be examined.*

Two days later, three hostages in their underwear were shot by the IDF as they waved a white flag after having fled from Hamas captivity.

The newspaper *Haaretz* calls itself liberal and is probably the only daily newspaper in Israel that still tries to give some semblance of objectivity and criticism, representing democracy and a certain moral standing, and gives space on its pages to Gideon Levy and Amira Hass, the most senior and established Israeli journalists who are openly opposed to the occupation. Two days after the three young men escaping from their guards were killed in Gaza, Maya Lecker wrote[71] that she wants "so much to believe Commander-in-Chief General Halevi" who said that the IDF does not shoot at people waving a white flag, but that she does not know "how many people believe the General".

Following this incident, the IDF launched an investigation which, after a short time, concluded that the soldiers should not be prosecuted because "there was no malice on their part". Can this be interpreted other than that it is perfectly acceptable – despite the General's words – to kill unarmed people waving a white flag? The soldiers mistook the person, but did not, according to the investigators, make a mistake in substance.

* * *

On Thursday, March 24, 2016, Ramzi al-Qasrawi and 'Abd al-Fatah a-Sharif attacked and injured a soldier with a knife at a checkpoint in Tel Rumeida, Hebron, on the West Bank. The soldier was injured. Soldiers shot al-Qasrawi dead instantly while a-Sharif was wounded and lying on the ground. A *B'tselem* activist films the entire scene. The video can be watched on *YouTube*, via the *B'tselem* page.[72] A large number of soldiers and several ambulances and other cars are on the scene taking care of the wounded soldier, but no one seems to notice a-Sharif lying on the street. Until one soldier exchanges a few words with another, perhaps his commander or an officer, unlocks his rifle and shoots a-Sharif in the head at close range. None of the other soldiers or officers act or interrupt what they are doing. The case received enormous international attention, thanks to *B'tselem's* camera.[73] The trial lasted ten months and the soldier was sentenced to 18 months in prison, later reduced to fourteen. He was imprisoned for nine months.

After he was sentenced, his family said it was as if "the court took the knife and stuck it in the back of all the soldiers". He was called "our king" by his supporters, and the right-wing parties and the settler movement thought his conviction was a complete travesty: "He is a hero!"

His "first months out of prison were a life of luxury. He received gifts and perks such as free cocktails and fully paid vacations", according to a survey by the news site *Mako*.[74]

Just the exception that proves the rule?

There are several testimonies that provide nuance to the picture of Hamas militiamen. Avital Alajem from Kibbutz Holit, a few kilometres east of Gaza, is still shocked and shaken as she tearfully describes militiamen burning and shooting and forcing her and her two young children to go to Gaza. Then she says: "I don't understand why they let us go when we got to the border. I don't understand why they saved my life and the lives of my two children. Then we went back and saw tanks and heard bombs. We just walked."[75]

In another video,[76] a woman identifying herself as Rotem is interviewed. She says that Hamas militiamen came into her house, and she said:

"- I have two children here. That was the first thing I said.

- In Hebrew?

- No, in English.

- They looked around and one of them said in English: 'Don't worry, I'm a Muslim, we won't hurt you.'"

She makes a gesture with her mouth, to show surprise or that she couldn't quite believe it. And then smiles a little.

"In a way it surprised me, but on the other hand it relieved me of a lot of worry. I was sitting down with my two children, and a militiaman came with a chair from the dining room. There was an armed man with us all the time in the room while the others went around the house. One of them saw some bananas on the sink and asked: Can I eat one? And I said 'Yes, that's fine.'"

She laughs.

- What did the children say, the interviewer asks.

- The oldest was more stressed, but the little one didn't care, but was busy with her iPad. They stayed in my house for a couple of hours and after that one of them closed the door when they left.

- Was that all? asks the interviewer, surprised.

- Yes, that's it.

Most of Hamas's hostages who have been released have said they were well treated.

Yocheved Lifschitz turned to shake hands with his jailer and told the press that they had been treated well: "When we got there, one of the guards said: 'We believe in the Koran and will not harm you'. They ate the same food as us and made sure we got the medicine we usually use".

This raised the ire of the Israeli government. "The Kan public broadcaster reports that Israeli PR experts are calling the decision to put Lifshitz in front of cameras a 'mistake.' In *Israel Hayom*, columnist Eddie Rothstein calls the interview a 'propaganda win for Hamas.'"[77]

Another released from Hamas captivity, Yarden Roman-Gat, testified on *60 Minutes* on December 18, 2023, about her experience in Gaza.[78] Her husband managed to hide in a ditch with their daughter and Yarden tried to play dead, but militiamen realized she was alive and dragged her to a car. She was wearing only pyjamas. "I was half-naked and even if they didn't have that idea, so…" She was afraid they would rape her but "their purpose was to take me to Gaza, and I wasn't raped".

When they entered Gaza, the street was full of people and "they couldn't resist showing me as a trophy".

She was never in the tunnels. "They took me to a house, and I was alone but never alone. There was always a guard, only men". She was given a hijab to cover her body. "I felt that this fabric was my only protection… but I was not hidden… I was seen all the time… they could do whatever they wanted with me; I was helpless."

The journalist asks if they saw her as a human being, if they wanted to protect her.

Yarden counters: "They didn't want to protect me. They wanted to preserve their trophy, but I think I managed to make them… I don't know, care somehow, and I think that helped me survive."

About the food she says: "Well, it was okay", and became worried when she heard that her sister-in-law was also in Gaza. She was afraid of the bombings. "It's a scary experience to be in a theater of war".

The journalist thinks that some of the hostages were given drugs to look happy when they were released, but Roman-Gat shakes her head and mumbles: "No".

Several other hostages released during the brief ceasefire in November told similar stories. One woman, Hin, and her daughter Ajam, who were kidnapped along with younger children Tal and Gal, told *Channel 12* that they told their guards they were worried something would happen to them, and were told,

"Don't worry, if something happens, we will die first." The daughter enjoyed arm-wrestling with her guards.[79]

Danielle Aloni and her daughter Emilia talked about the friendship that developed in detention with a migrant worker from Thailand, Nutthawaree Munkan. A letter in Hebrew has been circulated that Danielle allegedly wrote to thank Hamas for the support they gave to her daughter. Her relatives have dismissed it as propaganda, but she herself does not seem to have denied the authenticity of the letter. The Jewish independent, non-commercial news site *Forward* has an article on this.[80]

In line with this, sisters Erez and Sahar Kalderon said they were afraid of being killed by Israeli bombs, not by Hamas.[81]

Systematic sexual violence?

Two months after October 7, front pages around the world were suddenly filled with reports of sexual violence with headlines such as "Rape is a crime, but not if the victim is Jewish". The campaign culminated on December 28, 2023, when *The New York Times* published a long front-page article titled "*Screaming without words: How Hamas Weaponized Sexual Violence on Oct. 7*".[82] It was said to be the result of 150 interviews and two months of work, giving the impression that these are not isolated cases but systematic sexual violence. The article is about Gal and Nagi Abdush who were killed on October 7 at the Nova Festival. The authors claim that Gal was raped and that on the internet she is known as "the woman with the black dress" and has become a symbol of the brutal abuse of women. The article presents shocking details – unusual in a serious newspaper like *The New York Times*. The testimonies come from people who claim to have seen horrific rapes. It is intended to be moving, not least because of the large picture of Gal's family on the front page.

But the video cited as evidence is gone, the *Instagram* account is closed.

What are we to make of this? The impression that this was a case of "atrocity propaganda" was reinforced just a few days later, on January 1, 2024, when Nagi's brother Nissim Abdush appeared on Israel's *Channel 13*. For 14 minutes, he repeatedly denied that his brother's wife, Gal, had been raped. He explained that his brother Nagi had called him at 07:00 in the morning and said that his wife had been killed and that he was next to her body. Then he continued to communicate until 07:44 and never mentioned anything related to sexual abuse.[83]

Gal's sister Tali Barakha wrote on *Instagram*: "No one can know what Gal went through there! Nor what Nagi went through, but I cannot cooperate with those who say many things that are not true. I am asking you to stop spreading lies, there is a family and children after them, no one can know if it was rape or if she was burnt while she was alive. Have you gone mad? I spoke to Nagi personally! At seven o'clock, Gal was killed by those animals, and they shot her in the heart. Nagi lived until quarter to eight…"

Mondoweiss writes: "on December 29, the Israeli website 'YNET' published an interview with Etti Brakha, Gal Abdush's mother [only in Hebrew]. In the interview, the mother says that the family knew nothing about the sexual assault issue until the piece in the Times was published: 'We didn't know about the rape at all. We only knew after a New York Times journalist contacted us. They said they matched evidence and concluded that she had been sexually assaulted.'"

Electronic Intifada devoted a page to *The New York Times* article on January 9, 2024[84] (later on did Aljazeera the same[85]). They reviewed the witnesses, drawing the conclusion that they cannot be considered credible: "Their stories are not new", there is no corroboration or evidence and the stories changed over time. There are several posts on the internet that contradict the claims of these witnesses.

Another source is ZAKA, an ultra-orthodox Israeli body for the care of the deceased. ZAKA had previously published reports of beheaded babies, children being tied up and shot and burned, and a pregnant woman whose foetus was ripped from her stomach in the kibbutzim of Kfar Azza and Be'eri.[86] These stories were repeated by Cochav Elyakam-Lev, a lawyer and researcher at the Hebrew University of Jerusalem and the head of the Civil Commission on October 7 Crimes by Hamas against Women and Children, and turned out to be false.

Ali Abunimah in *The Electronic Intifada* writes: "The Times' 'investigation,' like previous similar stories by *The Washington Post, CNN, Haaretz, The Times of Israel* and others, does not confirm the existence of victims or physical or forensic evidence. Rather, it provides a litany of excuses for why there is no forensic evidence or crime scene photos – even though there was ample opportunity for authorities to collect them. Despite Israel saying there are tens of thousands of videos filmed on October 7, authorities have not claimed that a single one of them shows a rape or a sexual assault taking place – a glaring absence, given that Israel asserts that rape was used on a wide scale as a weapon of war."

On January 4, 2024, *Haaretz*[87] published an article showing that the police have very little knowledge of sexual assault after all and urged any victims to come forward and tell the police. This despite the fact that in December the IDF had forced hospitals to disclose the names of sexual assault victims, which the doctors protested against. But the fact is that it is unclear whether there are any people who have sought medical or psychiatric treatment for sexual abuse. It has been mentioned in the press that "a couple of people who have witnessed abuse have sought psychological support", but that is all. There is no autopsy or medical evidence. *The New York Times* writes: "The Israeli authorities have no shortage of video evidence from the Oct. 7 attacks. They have gathered hours of footage from Hamas body cameras, dash cams, security cameras and mobile phones showing Hamas terrorists killing civilians and many images of mutilated bodies. But Moshe Fintzy, a deputy superintendent and senior spokesman of Israel's national police, said, 'We have zero autopsies, zero,' making an O with his right hand."

Judith Levine, a journalist and author of the award-winning book *My Enemy, My Love: Man-Hating and Ambivalence in Women's Lives*, on the American news site *The Intercept*, strongly criticizes the reports of systematic rape on October 7, which she says are both absurd and conspiratorial:

> *The scandal that unfolded in early December was largely manufactured by right-wing pundits who until this moment didn't give a fig about rape. Mainstream media … could not resist feeding their audiences' prurience. Then some feminists took the bait, creating false moral distinctions — and strategic divisions between those who care about rape and those who also recognize the urgency of ending Israel's occupation and indiscriminate killing. Ultimately, the outcry distracts from the annihilation of Gaza and its people and lends Israel justification in perpetuating it. Needless to say, Prime Minister Benjamin Netanyahu is exploiting the opportunity.[88]*

The campaign claimed that the UN and international women's organizations were indifferent to the suffering of Jewish women — something that Levine shows in her article to be untrue. She lists all the initiatives, statements, and efforts that have been made to condemn the attack and tries to collect documentation on sexual violence for future trials. She refers to several press articles[89] criticizing Israel for lack of evidence and points out that

> *the right was first to portray these events as collaboration with terrorists. Fox News — the outfit that's paid Tucker Carlson and Laura Ingraham hundreds of millions of dollars to fan white paranoia and inform white Christians that Jews are replacing them — was now the great protector of Jewish dignity and life.*

The UN was not flexible enough, writes Levine, but the problem was that the Israeli organizations could not present any facts.

Dr. Cochav Elkayam-Levy appears in a long article in *Haaretz* as the champion, in Israel, of the work supporting victims of sexual assault, "The Scope of Hamas' Campaign of Rape Against Israeli Women Is Revealed, Testimony After Testimony".[90] The article starts saying that "what caused Cochav Elkayam-Levy to break down" was not seeing videos of abuses and violence, but "a brief phone conversation with Michal Herzog, the wife of Israel's president. "'Because it's like your mother calling and simply asking how you are doing,' explains Dr. Elkayam-Levy, her voice choking up immediately after she hangs up."

Cochav Elkayam-Levy was hard on international organizations:

They abandoned us in an immoral and terrible way. From the moment it dawned on me how much time and energy we were wasting trying to convince them – just to listen to us, just to believe us – the realization sunk in that these groups are not the 'address' where we can turn.

What makes her so disappointed is that they do not just believe her but want her to collect evidence and document the cases. Everything takes time, but investigating sexual abuse is particularly sensitive and requires careful and patient work. In the case of Rwanda, Human Rights Watch needed two years to gather enough information to issue a report proving widespread use of sexual violence during the 1994 genocide. But Elkayam-Levy wants the campaign now, not in two years.

She claims that,

Hamas carried out a campaign of rape and sexual abuse at many of the communities adjacent to the Gaza Strip that it attacked [but that] thus far, the commission has not taken testimony directly, but it will begin to do so soon. We have waited for relevant witnesses to give official evidence to the police, with the intention to then carry out in-depth interviews with them ourselves.

The only prove presented is from "the Shin Bet security service [which] has released recordings of at least two investigations of Nukhba [the Qassam brigades' elite units] terrorists who were asked whether they had been given specific orders to abuse women and children. Referring to the sex crimes, one of them said that the aim was 'to soil them, to rape them.' A second terrorist related that 'the commander said: You have to step on their heads. Cut off their heads. Do everything to them.' A military source cited by the daily Yedioth Ahronoth noted that 'the terrorists related that the aim of cutting off heads and rape was to sow fear and alarm in the Israeli public.'" I wonder if the *Shin Bet* has simply fabricated the confession (it wouldn't be the first time a security service has done so) or if it could be that the arrested Hamas men said something as overly ridiculous as a way of showing contempt for the Israeli secret police.

But there have been no reported cases of decapitated women. Cochav Elkayam-Levy describes her surprise and outrage when she says,

You are facing a bunch of respected women and telling them that shocking crimes were committed here. Am I the one who needs to provide the evidence for the terrorists' deeds? What kind of travesty is it that they are imposing the burden of proof on me?

It is a bit difficult to understand her. Who should provide evidence, if not Israeli organizations? She seems to think that the requirement to document and present evidence, which as a lawyer she should be very familiar with, is a sign of mistrust.

One argument that is repeated is that there was no time during the attack to gather evidence, which is not surprising, but even if the October 7 attack was completely unexpected and enormous in its scope, it is surprising that Israel, a modern and resourceful country, did not manage to obtain a single piece of evidence, no media evidence of sexual violence on October 7, no forensic evidence whatsoever.

Another argument is that most victims of sexual violence were killed and, according to their faith, they were buried quickly, and no one thought to collect evidence.

She seems somehow hurt:

We know that the vast majority of those who were harmed were also murdered. If there are survivors among those who were harmed, decades could go by before they gather the courage to talk about it. In the few cases in which someone else witnessed their suffering, I assume that then too questions will arise as to exactly what he saw and whether he is a reliable witness. I don't intend to participate in that game.

... "No, I do not allow myself to go there. Even with requests for numbers, I don't cooperate. They ask me: How many? How many? How many? There was one journalist here, a woman from a foreign news network, who drove me crazy. 'Are we talking about tens? Hundreds? Thousands?' I'm sorry. No. It would be irresponsible of me to cite a number."

One wonders what is so strange about wanting to know whether this is an isolated case or systematic violence. More difficult to understand is when she says that

the question we want to deal with is not whether something happened, but rather what type of crimes were committed, the systematic way they were committed and the orders to commit them. The question of the evidence that has been collected by the police, or not, is completely secondary. We aren't at all in a discussion of whether there were horrors here, or not. It is clear that any international body that will investigate them will get heaps of material that supports this. The aim is to reveal to humanity the depth of the suffering. The critical mass is the heart of the matter, and not this or that cross-section of an individual case.

Her attitude is very different from that of Physicians for Human Rights, which in November 2023 published a position paper, "Sexual and Gender Based and

Sexual Violence as a Weapon of War During the October 7 Attacks".[91] They repeated the same testimonies that have been circulated in the press and argue that a professional investigation is needed to determine whether the behaviour was systematic. They call for society to allocate resources to collect testimonies and break the culture of silence surrounding sexual abuse.

In a Zoom conference, several researchers speak about sexual violence and international rules.[92] Cochav Elkayam-Levy presents what is allegedly available on Hamas social media to prove various abuses, and then talks about people who claim to have seen abuses at the Nova festival and in kibbutzim. She talks about thousands of raped women, from babies to the elderly, mutilated and decapitated. Some of the descriptions are like something out of a horror movie. She says that Hamas men have been instructed to desecrate women as much as they can. Dvora Bauman, director of the Bat Ami Centre for Victims of Sexual Abuse in Israel, claims she knows that religious leaders gave Hamas men permission to abuse women, which their religion forbids. But she does not mention any proof or how she got this information.

What is documented is, in contrast, the minor scandal which arose in Israel when, in July 2016, Chief of Staff Gadi Eisenkot appointed Rabbi Eyal Karim as Chief Rabbi of the IDF, because he had said in 2012 that in war, actions were allowed that were normally forbidden, such as eating non-kosher food and raping women. He later explained that it was just a theological issue, but *The Times of Israel* wrote an article about it.[93]

What is clear is that the headline in *Haaretz* does not match the content of the text. "Testimony upon testimony", it claims – but no direct testimony is cited.

Elkayam-Levys organization, "Civil Commission on October 7 Crimes by Hamas against Women and Children" seem to have faded and been replaced by *The Association of Rape Crisis Centres in Israel* which published report "*Silent Cry Sexual Crimes in the October 7 War*"[94] (the wording *Silent Cry* could be an indirect reference to the New York Times article, *Screams Without Words*). The report presents four places where abuses can have occurred and refers to the same witnesses who have been reported in the press and on the internet, including ZAKA. The report may have been a step towards preparations for the UN mission that arrived in Israel on January 29, 2024, and stayed until February 14[95] The mission also visited Ramallah on the West Bank and met authorities and civil society organizations and witnesses. The day after the mission arrived in Israel, the Presidency of Israel made a public call[96] for victims and witnesses of sexual abuse to contact the authorities – clearly, a similar call by the Israeli police earlier (which Haaretz wrote about on January 4[97]) did not have any effect. The mission "did not meet with any survivor/victim of sexual violence from October 7 despite concerted efforts encouraging them to come forward."

Allegations of systematic sexual violence have been central to the argument justifying of Israel's genocide in Gaza and the country's authorities have worked hard on this. It is, therefore, important to carefully read the UN mission's report.

The report is 23 pages long and the investigations are organized around the four places that the report "Silent Cry" listed (Nova music festival, Road 232, Kibbutz Be'eri, and the military base Nahal Oz). The conclusion is that there are "reasonable grounds to believe that conflict-related sexual violence occurred during the October 7 attacks in multiple locations across Gaza periphery, including rape and gang rape, in at least three locations" but the report also admits that its findings must be seen in the light of "limited forensic evidence due to the large number of casualties and dispersed crime scenes in a context of persistent hostilities; the loss of potentially valuable evidence due to the interventions of some inadequately trained volunteer first responders; the prioritization of rescue operations and the recovery, identification, and burial of the deceased in accordance with religious practices, over the collection of forensic evidence. Further, a significant number of the recovered bodies had suffered destructive burn damage, which made the identification of potential crimes of sexual violence impossible."

The lack of trust against the UN and other international organizations in Israel is well known, both among the authorities and the (Jewish) citizens, but I was surprised that the lack of trust "was reportedly at an all-time low" and also extended to the national institutions in the country.

The report states several times that there are some indications that sexual violence can have occurred, that it cannot be ruled out, but in the specific cases one must conclude that the report's findings are concerning:

- in kibbutz Be'eri, "at least two allegations of sexual violence widely repeated in the media, were unfounded due to either new superseding information or inconsistency in the facts gathered. These included a highly publicized allegation of a pregnant woman whose womb had reportedly been ripped open before being killed, with her fetus stabbed while still inside her. Other allegations, including of objects intentionally inserted into female genital organs, could not be verified by the mission team due in part to limited and low-quality imagery." (page 5)

- "In kibbutz Kfar Azza, while reports of conflict-related sexual violence, including at least one instance of rape, could not be verified, available circumstantial evidence may be indicative of some forms of sexual violence." (page 5)

- "On Road 232, credible information based on witness accounts describe an incident of the rape of two women by armed elements. Other reported instances of rape could not be verified in the time allotted. The mission team also found a pattern of bound naked or partially naked bodies from the waist down, in some cases tied to structures including trees and poles, along Road 232. In kibbutz Re'im, the mission team further verified an incident of the rape of a woman outside of a bomb shelter and heard of other allegations of rape that could not yet be verified." (page 5)

- "In the Nahal Oz military base, the mission team reviewed reports of sexual violence including a case of rape and genital mutilation, neither of which could be verified. With respect to the latter instance, while the forensic analysis reviewed injuries to intimate body parts, no discernible pattern could be identified, against either female or male soldiers." (page 5)

More surprisingly, the report is more conclusive on the hostages in Gaza: "With respect to hostages, the mission team found clear and convincing information that some have been subjected to various forms of conflict-related sexual violence including rape and sexualized torture and sexualized cruel, inhuman and degrading treatment and it also has reasonable grounds to believe that such violence may be ongoing."

The mission notes in several places in the report the large quantities of bodies with *destructive burn damage* (pages 1, 2, 3, 4, 5, 6, and 7) which can reasonably only refer to anything else than cases similar to the charred bodies shown in the IDF's short video [98] which can only be explained as the result of heavy artillery (missiles or grenades from tanks, drones, helicopters or aircraft), weapons which Hamas does not possess.

The report reads: "It must be noted that witnesses and sources with whom the mission team engaged adopted over time an increasingly cautious and circumspect approach regarding past accounts, including in some cases retracting statements made previously. Some also stated to the mission team that they no longer felt confident in their recollections of other assertions that had appeared in the media." (page 16)

The diplomatic language in the passage below about kibbutz Be'eri somewhat disguises very serious allegations: *some evidence had been fabricated and one crime scene had been manipulated.* It is difficult to understand this in any other way than that the Israeli authorities themselves or through individuals or organizations have *lied and purposefully tried to deceive international opinion with the purpose of justifying a genocide.*

"At least two of the allegations of sexual violence previously reported were determined by the mission team to be unfounded, due to either new superseding information or inconsistency in the information gathered, including first responder testimonies, photographic evidence and other information. These included the allegation of a pregnant woman whose womb had reportedly been ripped open before she was killed, with her foetus stabbed while still inside her. Another such account was the interpretation initially made of the body of a girl found separated from the rest of her family, naked from the waist down. It was determined by the mission team that the crime scene had been altered by a bomb squad and the bodies moved, explaining the separation of the body of the girl from the rest of her family. Allegations of objects found inserted in female genital organs also could not be verified by the mission team due in large part to the limited availability and low quality of imagery." (page 17)

Moreover: "In the medicolegal assessment of available photos and videos, no tangible indications of rape could be identified." (page 19)

"The reviewed photos and videos revealed widespread mutilation of bodies, involving both attempted and actual decapitation, numerous gunshot wounds, and various other forms of extensive violence. The medicolegal assessment of available photos and videos revealed multiple corpses with injuries, predominantly gunshot wounds, including to intimate body parts such as breasts and genitalia. Because in most instances additional injuries were also seen on other body parts, no discernible pattern of genital mutilation could be established." (page 19) So, massive and spread violence, but no signs of systematic sexual violence.

Some people have said that evidence can got lost on the internet, but the report says that "While it is possible that digital evidence may have been posted and then removed from official channels and social media profiles, possibly due to concerns by the various groups that it may be incriminating, it is the view of the mission team that, had clear digital evidence of sexual violence or orders to commit sexual violence been circulated in the mainstream, it would have likely been discovered given the volume of the information posted online and further recirculated, making the removal of all trace of such material unlikely." (page 19)

"Hamas and other Palestinian armed groups, including but not limited to the Palestinian Islamic Jihad and Popular Resistance Committees, have claimed responsibility for the attacks of October 7, 2023. In its report '*Our Narrative: Operation Al-Aqsa Flood*', Hamas has however denied claims of harm against civilians, including the commission of rape. Given the mission was not investigative, it did not gather information and/or draw conclusions on attribution of alleged violations to specific armed groups. Such attribution would require a fully-fledged investigative process." (page 20)

The mission did not had great ambitions regarding the situation of Palestinians in Israeli prisons because the Palestinians, in contrast to Israel, cooperate with the UN. Anyhow, the report states: "As of February 2024, according to the Israel Prison Service, there are nearly 9,000 Palestinians in Israeli custody, including 3,484 administrative detainees (39 per cent) held without trial. The interviewed persons alleged that the conditions of detention of Palestinian men and women are cruel, inhuman and degrading treatment, including increasingly sexual violence, invasive body searches of detainees, touching of intimate areas and forced unveiling of women wearing Hijab; beatings, including in the genital areas; threats of rape against women and threats of rape against female family members (wives, sisters, daughters) in the case of men; inappropriate naked search, prolonged forced nudity, also during interrogation and transfer to other prisons. Moreover, soldiers circulate pictures of women detainees and women are deprived of menstruation products. They also reported sexual harassment and threats of rape during house raids – including at night – and at checkpoints. They also highlighted intimidation, including threats of rape, if conditions of detention were reported or publicly disclosed after liberation. While no instances of rape were reported, Palestinian women's organizations consistently stressed that in addition to intimidation and insecurity, the high level of stigmatization, conservative cultural norms and the power imbalance in the context of occupation impedes reporting of sexual violence.

Both Israeli and Palestinian civil society organizations reported to the mission team that since October 7, 2023, the prison authorities have severely limited the access of independent humanitarian bodies to detention facilities to monitor the conditions of detention and address any abuses. They also stressed that information on Palestinians from Gaza detained in Israel was difficult to obtain and raised concerns that, due to ongoing hostilities and humanitarian crisis, there is very limited information on whether sexual violence may be occurring in Gaza." (page 21. The text has been shortened slightly to ease the reading).

Two other important remarks in the report:

- "The mission team did not consider for the purpose of this report accounts collected by Israeli intelligence bodies, including those related to interrogations of alleged perpetrators, despite some being offered, due to the mission team's inability in the time allotted to establish the due process rights of the accused person and adequate authentication."(page 9) On plain language: testimony obtained during interrogation are not reliable because can be made under duress.

- "It must be noted that the information gathered by the mission team was in a large part sourced from Israeli national institutions. This is due to the absence of United Nations entities operating in Israel, as well as the lack of cooperation by the State of Israel with relevant United Nations bodies with an investigative mandate."(page 14) Two comments on this: first, Israel does not cooperate with the UN (Israel's relationship with the UN is extremely conflicted). Second, it is necessary to consider that the statements from one party in the conflict can be partial – this is evident to anyone, except Western journalists and politicians.

In conclusion:

"there are reasonable grounds to believe that conflict-related sexual violence occurred at several locations across the Gaza periphery, including in the form of rape and gang rape, during the October 7, 2023, attacks. Credible circumstantial information, which may be indicative of some forms of sexual violence, including genital mutilation, sexualized torture, or cruel, inhuman, and degrading treatment, was also gathered.

With regards to the hostages, the mission team found clear and convincing information that some hostages taken to Gaza have been subjected to various forms of conflict-related sexual violence and has reasonable grounds to believe that such violence may be ongoing.

The mission team was unable to establish the prevalence of sexual violence and concludes that the overall magnitude, scope, and specific attribution of these violations would require a fully-fledged investigation." (pages 21, 22)

The Israeli authorities rush to claim that the report confirmed systematic sexual violence, but this is not the case. The report states that it cannot be ruled out that sexual violence, including rape, has occurred, but the report does not find convincing evidence to support the claims that it has happened. The concrete cases presented to the team were one after another dismissed as not credible or outright false, including outright fabrication in some cases. Sexual violence is common in armed conflicts. In some cases (former Yugoslavia, Democratic Republic of Congo) it has been proven that sexual violence was systematically used as a weapon to demoralise the enemy and the population. The mission does not draw any such conclusion. On the contrary it could not find any pattern of systematic sexual violence, in spite there being indications that sexual violence may have happened.

In fact, the report is much more concrete and clearer about the violence, including sexualized violence, that Israel's police and military perpetrate against the thousands of Palestinian prisoners in Israeli detention.

The spokesperson of kibbutz Be'eri, Michal Paikin, has denied the allegations that the sisters Y. and N. Sharabi were raped. "No, they just – they were shot. I'm saying 'just', but they were shot and not subjected to sexual abuse." The family said that the girls were killed together with their mother and not in a bedroom as has been stated.[99]

ZAKA

ZAKA, an ultra-religious rescue service in Israel, plays a central role in the atrocity propaganda (see Appendix III, page 155) and it is important to try to understand what it is.

There are reports that ZAKA volunteers mixed up the remains of different people. ZAKA excuses themselves by saying that they do not have medical expertise, which is a very strange thing to say for an organization dedicated to taking care of dead people after accidents and attacks. It is not difficult to understand that one could use volunteers who are not medically trained but such an organization, authorised to act in these circumstances by the government and the IDF, should be able to guarantee at least that their volunteers can judge whether they are capable of handling the situation they are faced with or not, and if necessary, call for help. (Israel is not a poor forgotten country – on the contrary, Israel excels with its Nobel laureates, modern industries, and research institutes. Playing small and helpless does not quite fit).

ZAKA's Yossi Landau "broke down"[100] shortly after the October 7 attack during a presentation at the Jerusalem Press Club when he described "a pregnant woman in Kibbutz Be'eri in a 'big puddle of blood, face down.'–'Her stomach was butchered open,' Landau said. 'The baby that was connected to the cord was stabbed.'" He spoke of two small children who were tied up with their parents and killed, an eye missing, fingers cut off. "'The terrorists were having a ball', with Palestinian militants devouring a holiday meal set out by the family", he said.

"Long after Landau's emotional recollections were replayed, repeated, cited, and quoted in the global media, a problem emerged: No one could find any evidence that the two massacres ever took place — in Be'eri or elsewhere.", wrote Arun Gupta in *The Intercept*[101].

> *In the case of the butchered mother and foetus, the Israeli newspaper Haaretz concluded the killing 'simply didn't happen.' As for the tortured family, no one killed in Be'eri matches Landau's account. The one brother and sister to die in the kibbutz were 12-year-old twins, killed when an Israeli general ordered a tank to fire on a house where Hamas militants were holding them hostage. Nevertheless, Landau told these stories unchecked in interviews and press conferences. Landau spread his tales far and wide with little pushback — telling similar stories on camera to CNN, Fox News, and the Media Line, and at an outdoor press conference. Even after reporters showed his accounts lacked any substantiation, news organizations continued to let him off the hook. The New York Times recently interviewed Landau as part of a profile about Zaka, but it did not mention either of his atrocity stories.*

In spite of all allegations against ZAKA the press keeps on citing them. On January 15, 2024, *The New York Times* published an idyllic portrait of the organization.[102]

It seems quite clear that ZAKA has used its work on October 7 as a fundraising campaign. "ZAKA reportedly turned massacre sites into a 'war room for donations', used corpses as fundraising props, spread accounts of atrocities that never happened, and botched forensics that are central to Israel's claim that Hamas carried out a premeditated campaign of mass rape."

ZAKA personnel and soldiers from IDF:s Military Rabbinate did not handle corpses carefully, according to *Haaretz*.

> *When soldiers trained in recovery were finally let in the second week after the attack, they were alarmed by Zaka's actions.[...] Zaka volunteers seemed less intent on bagging bodies than grabbing money". According to Haaretz, Zaka failed to document remains, put parts from different bodies in the same bag, and did not collect all the remains in homes or in the field. Zaka volunteers apparently did find time to rewrap already bagged remains in material that 'prominently displayed the Zaka logo'.*

'I did not take pictures because we are not allowed to take pictures', said

Yossi Landau to The New York Times, a ZAKA volunteer. 'In retrospect, I regret it' … Yet these are Landau's assertions, as is his claim that Zaka volunteers can't take pictures of the dead. Haaretz reported that Zaka 'released sensitive and graphic photos' from massacre sites. There is news footage, showing remains being carried on stretchers, labelled 'Videos taken onsite by Zaka volunteers.' And Greiniman, the Zaka deputy commander, has bragged at least three times of 'all the pictures and all the evidence, we have everything to prove it' — but nothing has ever been publicly produced"

writes Gupta in the mentioned article in *The Intercept*. In the 1980s, ZAKA founder Meshi-Zahav led an extreme ultra-Orthodox movement called Keshet, which, on religious grounds, protested against archaeological excavations and autopsies. ZAKA's history is a string of scandals not least after their founder and leader was accused of sexual abuse and killed himself at the time the organization was heavily in debt.

ZAKA is not unique in lying. Liza Rozovsky and Josh Breiner wrote in Haaretz [103] about another case of false accusations, this time by: "The officer, Lt. Col. Guy Basson, deputy commander of the Kfir Brigade, claimed that eight infants were murdered in the communal nursery, and that an Auschwitz survivor called Genia was also murdered. These incidents described in the interview, which aired on Saturday night, never happened."

The Editing of a Massacre

Several major media outlets have published edited productions with the aim of providing a picture of the events and helping readers and viewers to bring some sort of order to the flood of information. We will analyze a couple of them.

Quite often, the image or video does not match what the text or speaker is saying. A good example of this is a *CNN* story on October 10, 2023, under the headline "*Evidence suggests militiamen at music festival threw grenade into shelter*" but the article is illustrated with an aerial photo showing a large area of burnt ground where the cars were parked. You can see some abandoned cars and three excavators.[104] The text reads:

> *The bullet holes and empty shell casings littered inside a bomb shelter near the music festival attacked on Saturday indicate that Hamas militants threw a grenade and opened fire at civilians sheltering inside, according to a weapons expert. CNN visited the bomb shelter on Monday and saw several empty shell casings on the floor, in addition to bullet holes high up on the walls. The military expert who accompanied CNN in the shelter concluded that the location of the holes, in addition to their height, pattern and size, were caused by gunfire. CNN is not naming the weapons expert because the individual is in a conflict zone in Israel.*

Mentioning a weapons expert in this context seems superfluous. If there are empty shells and holes in the walls, you don't need to be an expert to draw conclusions, but the article does not show a photo of shells in a shelter and bullet holes on the wall. I have heard and read it repeated by journalists in written texts and TV broadcasts. There is a film of a shelter where people were killed, but the pictures of other shelters are not convincing. The shelters mentioned on several news sites are small structures next to bus stops, meant to be used in case of a rocket attack while waiting for the bus. They are about the size of the bus shelter, ten by five or six feet. Most are painted with graffiti on the outside. This raises the suspicion that it is something that happen once and then took wing and was repeated.

"*Dash cam shows Hamas militiamen firing around during the attack on the music festival*",[105] is the title of a video in which journalist Anderson Cooper visits the festival site and interviews IDF spokesman Daniel Hagari, who, in a field full of cars, some of them severely damaged and burned, says: "They were waiting here with a machine gun".

That can't be right. Josh Breiner in *Haaretz*, November 18,[106] says: "*Israeli Security Establishment: Hamas Likely Didn't Have Advance Knowledge of Nova Festival*". The festival was scheduled to run from Thursday to Friday, and the organizers decided to extend the festival by an extra day as late as two days before the event began. The police investigation "reveals that the terrorists intended to infiltrate Re'im and other kibbutzim near the Gaza border" and that the decision to attack the festival was spontaneous. "The first terrorists arrived at the location from Route 232 [east of the festival area], and not from the direction of the border [which is to the west]… In a video from one of the terrorists' bodycams, he is heard asking a captured citizen for directions to Re'im." The police determined that the festival ended half an hour before the first shooting was heard. There were about 4,400 people and the vast majority managed to escape after the decision to ask people to leave was made four minutes after the rocket attack started, according to police.

Fifty-four seconds into Anderson Cooper's video, the camera shows some objects on the ground: an umbrella, some bags and plastic bags, a sleeping bag, an envelope, obviously people have left in a hurry and there is disorder but there are no signs of violence and there are no blood stains. The journalist says, "the bodies and body parts of the dead have been removed but their possessions are scattered around. The carnage is clear, burnt cars, bullet holes, blood stains on seats". The camera shows no blood stains on the ground but a car with a bullet hole and the damaged seat and broken glass, but it is unclear whether what is shown are blood stains. Some cars are completely demolished, not just burnt. Half a minute later, the journalist says that the IDF took some dash cams showing Hamas men walking around for hours shooting freely. The camera shows a man firing a shot. The speaker says: "This one shows a bloody hostage being led away by a militiaman and under a car another man is seen hiding and moving slightly and stops. An armed man comes up to him and shoots him at point blank range in the head or body."

The video shows a man (A) armed with a rifle. He does not have the Hamas green headband but is wearing a vest that could be a protective vest. The hostage (B) does not appear to be bloodied and walks on his own as the man pushes him in front of him. Then another armed civilian comes up to the man under the car and points the rifle at him, but the film ends (the same sequence, but longer, on *Human Rights Watch* home page, shows that the man is shot). Three men are then shown wearing military clothing and a headband that does not appear to be Hamas green. The same scene can be seen in another presentation by CNN,[107] which shows the beginning of the incident: (A) is seen firing a few shots and then he pulls (B) up and pushes him in front of him.

IDF spokesperson Daniel Hagari says: "I don't understand how people can explain this. I don't have the words… and running away on motorcycles… with girls to Gaza!" Hagari makes a face of disgust as he emphatically says: "*with girls to Gaza!*"

Another video extensively shared on the internet shows Noah Argamani being picked up on a small motorcycle by two unarmed civilians who drive off (there is also an article on *Wikipedia*[108]). Some unarmed youths are seen taking Noah on a motorcycle and soon afterwards, her boyfriend, Avinathan Or, is forced by two unarmed young men on foot, presumably to a car to take him to Gaza. Noah and Avinathan are hostages in Gaza. Noah appeared in a video released by Hamas together with two other hostages, Etai Firsky and Yosi Sherabi asking the government to stop the war. Here, Noah announces that Etai Firsky and Yosi Sherabi were killed by the bombing. *MiddleEastEye's* correspondent in Beersheba[109] interviewed the distraught Noah's father, Yakov Argamani. He describes how shocked he was when he saw the video of his daughter being taken on a motorcycle into Gaza. "A little later I saw another clip and she was a little calmer in that one and drinking water… I believe that she is protected. That there are people among them who have a heart, people who are merciful." Yakov expresses hope that he will soon meet his daughter "and so that we together can think about what is best for us and also for them. They are suffering too. They are being battered too. We have to stop this killing between us and them, so that there can be real peace between these two countries once and for all."

The next clip in Anderson Coopers video is the same as the one on the *Human Rights Watch's* report from October 18. Some armed men around a building, a man on the ground, they scream at him and a man kicks him. One militia man throws a grenade into the building; moments later a man runs out and the militiamen shoot at him him and a few moments later there is an explosion inside the room.

After this, the video shows a small shelter packed with people. The journalist says that "you can hear panic in the voices" but the voices do not seem to be overly agitated. "Noam Cohen said that Hamas men repeatedly threw grenades inside the shelter, and people inside were blown apart. It's one of the most horrific images we've seen." A second later we see a man's leg blackened, like soot, but not bloody and a wounded woman lying down and reaching out to people around her (who seem to be unharmed). It is difficult to see, there could be more people lying down or injured. Then the camera shows an image from below, showing Noam Cohen's face: "Noam Cohen survived hiding under the body parts. Here he is, terrified, paralyzed", says the journalist. In another presentation of the same video, you can see a man's leg with some wounds, but the videos don't show blood on the walls or the floor.

The video goes on showing a similar shelter – the same opening without a door with large graffiti images on the outside wall, in this case a dog and some flowers. A blanket hangs over the opening. The reporter's voice says: "Shelter in the city of Alumin. Someone hung a curtain over the door, but nothing can hide the smell when you enter… blood on the wall… bullet holes… from grenades that were thrown in." The reporter enters with a mobile phone as a light and shines it on the wall where there is black graffiti and some stains on the wall. He seems to be gagging. There are three holes in the bare concrete wall. No blood is visible, mostly dirt. The next picture gives a clear impression. Garbage, shit, rubbish, plastic, old clothes, bottles, garbage bags. A turquoise piece of cloth that should be bloody had there been a massacre in this cramped space, but the cloth is clean. It appears to have been a hangout for drunks or junkies or used as a "garbage room". The shelter shown earlier appeared to be larger and was at ground level. This shelter is completely dark.

The last scene shows several cars that are not only burnt out but completely destroyed, demolished, as if a tank had run over them.

A week later, *CNN* published an edited presentation: "How a rave festival to celebrate life turned into a horrific massacre",[110] using several short clips from the video commented on above. The presentation combines text and images and is obviously intended to evoke emotions about the Supernova music festival where some 364 people allegedly were killed. The first completely black page warns: "This story contains video and images of violence. Viewer discretion is advised. Many of the videos include disturbing audio". You can choose to play it with or without sound. It's effective and makes you wonder what's coming. Throughout the presentation, the screen is black, the text is white and most videos, usually 7 to 10 seconds long, run in a small window on the right. Despite all the warnings, hardly any violence is shown. Many allegations could easily have been supported with images, but such images are not shown.

After three short video clips, there is a longer text that begins by saying that the attack "was not only highly coordinated, but designed to kill as many people as possible", which we have seen does not correspond to what actually happened because Hamas did not know about the festival, and also by the images of armed and unarmed civilians taking hostages.

Josh Breiner writes in the aforementioned *Haaretz* article that "the investigation also indicates that an IDF combat helicopter that arrived at the scene and fired at terrorists there apparently also hit some festival participants." This is consistent with two observations: larger areas of burnt land and demolished cars. Josh Breiner's article is illustrated by a photo with the following text: "Burned cars belonging to participants of the Nova Festival, after the Hamas attack of October 7. Credit: Eliyahu Hershkovitz". The photo shows at least 50–60 cars; the 10–20 in the foreground are completely demolished (there are many similar photographs of completely demolished cars in other articles and video presentations). Such destruction could hardly have been caused by Hamas, let alone Palestinian civilians entering Israel spontaneously through the breaches in the barrier.

The text and images may lead the viewer to believe that it was the rocket attack that caused the music to stop, but as we have seen, the police investigation shows that the music stopped half an hour before the shooting started.

Noam Cohen in the shelter

The short video clip from the shelter (in this largely edited presentation) has the following explanatory text:

> *About 30 people were inside… [Noam Cohen] filmed several sequences afterwards, his face is bloody and shows the horrible scene inside afterwards… Minutes later there was a huge explosion, gunfire, and several grenades were thrown through the door, killing most of the people inside. 'To survive I kept myself under the bodies of the dead, with body parts,' Cohen said. Metadata confirmed the time and place.*

Noam Cohen was interviewed by J. Street on October 12, 2023.[111] He talks about his experiences in the shelter. Cohen says the music stopped after Hamas began the rocket attack and then he went into a bomb shelter:

> *after a few minutes we got hit with RPG… most of the shelter collapsed on us; a lot of pieces from the shelter, and we heard a lot of shootings… 5, 10, 20 people shooting at the shelter… people were climbing on each other… threw a grenade inside the shelter the kind of grenades that throw pieces all over… like four grenades and they thought they killed everyone… we were like 30 people inside, only five or six were getting from it alive… what*

I did was to cover myself with dead bodies to survive. They got inside the shelter and just shoot, shoot everyone, and a lot of bullets got inside my legs; right now, I can't really walk; both of my legs are with bullets and pieces from the grenade. One is in bad condition – all the muscle is ripped and one is in a better... then like after 40 minutes of them shooting us and do it, they went, they got off there and... I don't know if you saw the videos but it was people stacked on each other like in a huge pile and I was in the bottom so all the shots didn't affect me...

[Someone whispers to him]

I'll try to make it not too scary, but it was like a horror movie, like, you think, people with body parts, a lot of girls, a lot of my friends there. Then I just ran out of this shelter. I saw a car, I got inside and drove like 100 metres... [to] a small town of Jews... they took care of me, gave me pills for pain and trauma and they took care of me... Terrorists tried to enter the kibbutz, but there were armed people there, not the army, but they were able to defend us.

The details could be wrong, like how many people were firing and for how long, what kind of weapons were used, the time and place. But even if I want to believe Cohen, it is striking that he contradicts himself about his own body. First, one of his legs is so badly injured that he can't walk, and a minute later he says that the shooting didn't injure him because he was under all the bodies. It is, of course, difficult to judge what his "selfie" shows, certainly fear and horror, but if he had been injured in the leg by shrapnel from a grenade and by bullets, it is hard to believe that he would then stand up and take a selfie.

The video also does not show any parts of the building "collapsing on us". There are one or two wounded persons on the floor but no blood on the walls or ceiling and more than five or six seem to be alive, at least after this attack.

An American girl, Lee Sasi, was in another shelter and tells a similar story. The same presentation by CNN reads:

Sasi said there were about 35 to 40 people huddled together. Hamas militants fired weapons and threw grenades into it, killing the vast majority, she said. Among the dead was her uncle. 'We had to bury ourselves under these dead corpses to protect ourselves from these grenades that were hitting, and from the rifles and the RPG (rocket-propelled grenades),' she said, adding that her cousin, who fled to a different shelter, also died there. Sasi sent three videos that she filmed at the shelter, including one disturbing clip that showed her hiding under bodies. CNN geolocated the structure to the junc-

tion outside of Be'eri, the nearest community to the festival ground, which was also attacked by Hamas.

There are several articles about Lee Sasi where she describes brains and stomachs erupting. She said: "It was Holocaust 2.0… Hamas wants to wipe all Jews off the face of the earth… they laughed when they killed us." Only in some of the many interviews with her on the internet is a sequence from inside the room shown – barely a second long, with a lot of masking of the images, so that it is impossible to get an idea of what is shown. Some of the interviews are illustrated with the same videos found in several presentations. The shelter where she says a massacre took place shows no visible damage on the outside and you see a couple of soldiers walking around and one of them patting the other's gun. The video says that Lee Sasi took pictures of herself under all the bodies, but no such pictures are shown. Another sequence clearly shows how remarkably careless and even reckless the major media are in handling the information.

In the CNN presentation, there is a box with the following text accompanying a video: "At least 10 gunmen shoot at the vehicle, the windshield cracking with each shot." The video filmed with a camera inside the car shows a single man shooting. A bullet strikes the windshield, leaving a small whitish "stain" and after three to four seconds the windshield cracks.

It is a bit difficult to understand why Hamas would waste RPGs, a weapon designed to stop tanks and larger military vehicles, on a group of people inside a shelter. One would have expected to see a picture of serious damage to the shelter itself. In various videos I have seen at least five different shelters, most of them next to bus stops, as in this case, but none of them show signs of a major explosive impact. The graffiti adorning them is either somewhat fresh or weathered, but nothing else and none shows impacts or damages. The similarities in the stories of Lee Sasi and Noam Cohen are striking: both were lying under bodies and body parts; both came under fire from small arms and RPGs and survived grenade explosions in very small shelters measuring between 50 and 60 square feet, full of people. Both refer to videos of themselves lying under piles of bodies of the dead. There is a video showing a massacre in such a shelter, but the other shelters shown do not show any evidence of massacres, casings, rests of grenades nor blood stains on the walls or floor.

Another question that arises is why there is no data or interviews with other people who may have been injured there.

What does Hamas want?
What do the Palestinians want?

Terese Cristiansson interviewed Hamas spokesperson Osama Hamdan on December 20, 2023, on the Swedish *TV4* channel.[112] He explained that the military objectives had been achieved faster than expected:

Nobody was talking about Palestine. The goal was to start to talk about the rights of the Palestinian people and the central Palestinian demand for statehood… Suddenly, President Biden says that the solution is a Palestinian state. It's a huge change… I am in charge of my people, and we have to achieve the goals of the Palestinians which are an independent Palestinian state with Jerusalem as its capital and having the Palestinian refugees return to their homes.

Asked if he feels any guilt for the many dead civilians in Gaza, and his answer is "What I feel is that there must be an end to the occupation because if there was no occupation these people would not be killed, they would have normal lives." The journalist asks if there will be a solution for the prisoners. Hamdan says that "after the ceasefire, the end of the siege of Gaza, we will start to talk to Israel through mediators. Our goal is clear. We want the Palestinian prisoners free from the Israeli jails, and when this happens, we will send back the prisoners of war."

Many have speculated that one of Hamas's goals was to sabotage the Abraham Accords, the establishment of diplomatic relations between the Arab states and Israel (Bahrain, the United Arab Emirates, Sudan, and Morocco have already normalized relations with Israel), and especially to hinder the rapprochement between the Saudis and Israel, which the US worked hard to achieve.

Others have suggested that the attack may be a reaction to the violence and incursions in the West Bank and Jerusalem and the provocations at the Al-Aqsa Mosque on the Dome of the Rock, but the attack must have required a long time in the planning. October 7 may have been chosen in view of the 1973 war, which started on October 6, 1973, just over 50 years earlier, which Israel regards as a major defeat that forced it to give up the Sinai Peninsula.

Whether they were deliberate targets or not is difficult to determine, but the October 7 attack has already had some other results:

- It has shattered Israel's central strategy: deterrence. Hamas managed to neutralize the IDF's communications system, hit the IDF's Gaza Division headquarters, and take control of the Gaza Envelope, which for a few hours was entirely in Hamas's hands. In some kibbutzim, Hamas managed to hold on for up to two or three days. Not very long, one might think, and in the end, they were killed along with their hostages.

- A direct consequence of this is that the Israeli people's faith in their army has been seriously compromised. Numerous accounts speak of "people in the south hiding in safe rooms, under beds and in wardrobes, hoping and believing that help was coming; that in this kind of situation, the army and police would come to their rescue within minutes. But no one came".[113]

- It has sent a message to the Israelis that they are not invincible, that there is a price to pay for maintaining the occupation.

- It is difficult to estimate the economic damage that Hamas's attacks will have on Israel's economy, both directly, as many people have had to leave their jobs to fight in Gaza and the north. But more importantly, indirectly, by calling into question Israel's big showpiece – weapons, military products, and systems, and not least the surveillance and control systems it has tested in its huge laboratory (seven million Palestinians in Gaza, the West Bank, East Jerusalem, and within its own borders). Israel has been touting itself as a world leader in mass control systems: walls and fences, roadblocks, and crossings, but Hamas attack has shown that it was possible to tear these down, which could make prospective customers think twice before buying these systems for big money.

- Major General Eitan Dangot is perhaps the first person in the world to admit that Hamas has managed to administer Gaza as a proper state. In a long interview with *i24NEWS*[114] he mentions several times the "Hamas state" as the enemy that must be destroyed, annihilated. It is a recognition of Hamas's capacity to govern, even if it is under very peculiar circumstances, and the Palestinian Authority in Ramallah is probably green with envy. It is not difficult to agree with the General. Whatever one thinks of Hamas and the way they exercise power, it has shown that it can run a functioning society and even raise an army capable of doing what no Arab state has ever done: wage war inside Israeli territory.

- Hamas has emerged as a force to be reckoned with, truly standing up to Israel. Hamas has shown that even under the difficult conditions created by nearly two decades of blockade, it can strike at Israel. Hamas's prestige among Palestinians has skyrocketed, and the Palestinian Authority has correspondingly lost support.

- To the entire Arab and Muslim world, Hamas appear to be heroes, and the governments of these countries cannot ignore this, much as they may detest Hamas. Israel's indiscriminate bombing of Gaza, broadcast live on *Aljazeera*, will affect the entire region for decades. It is difficult to assess how, but the people of Arab countries have seen what no one thought was possible. Israel's response will have a huge impact far beyond Palestine.

- The Israeli answer to the October 7 attack has utterly isolated Israel and USA in the world and showed the real face of Western liberalism.[115]

Did Hamas intend to kill as many people as possible?

Is there evidence that Hamas's aim was to systematically kill and injure as many people as possible and destroy as much as possible? In the interview on Swedish *TV4*, senior Hamas leader, Osama Hamdan said:

on the military level it was according to the plan. Maybe it took less time than it was expected. And that created a new situation. When all the military surrounding Gaza fell, everyone from Gaza went outside to what they consider their own land and at that moment a chaos happened. No one can guarantee what happened exactly. This was not part of the military operation.

A significant part of Gaza's population are refugees from other parts of what was once the British Mandate of Palestine, mainly from southern areas. Hamas has consistently argued that taking civilian hostages to Gaza was not an objective and they cannot take responsibility for what Gazan civilians did that day. This seems to be in line with what former Israeli Prime Minister Neftali Bennet said 12 minutes into an interview with the *BBC*[116] on December 20, 2023: "We know that it was the third wave of the attack that was the most violent, that was when rape and other violence… was carried out by civilians."

As we have seen, in the area of the Nova Festival, some unarmed youths and other armed men took hostages to Gaza, which must be part of the "third wave". There is evidence that several civilians were killed by Hamas, but it is unclear how many and under what circumstances. It is also clear that Israeli planes, helicopters, and tanks killed civilians, and it can hardly be disputed that some people died in crossfire.

Regarding the claims of mass rape, Hamdan said on Swedish *TV4*:

Some women were taken to Gaza, and they were later released and went home. None of them talked about sexual assault or rape. During the attack itself, it was a tight situation with little time. If they were not abused in Gaza [when there was] time and opportunity, I think that it didn't happen [during the attack] when it was a hurry. I don't defend such things, and if it happened, those who did that will be questioned. No doubt about it.

The New Yorker published an article on October 13 based on an interview with Mousa Abu Marzouk, a senior political leader of Hamas:[117]

Abu Marzouk appeared eager to open negotiations over the release of hostages. He declared that Hamas was ready to release any women, children, or elderly captives, in addition to citizens of other countries—if Israel ceased its military campaign. 'The innocent people who were imprisoned, we will not keep them,' he told us. (Whether Hamas's military leaders concur remains to be seen.) He indicated that Hamas might seek to swap some Israeli soldiers for Palestinians being held in Israeli jails, but added, 'It's too early to talk about swaps'.

Four days later, on October 17, *The Cradle* reported that

Al-Qassam Brigades, Abu Ubaida, confirmed that [Hamas] hold 'about 200' prisoners of war [Hamas means that soldiers and civilians with weapons are prisoners, not hostages] *and pledged to release all foreign nationals when the Israeli army stops the constant bombardment of Gaza. 'We cannot currently reveal the complete and accurate number of captives in the Gaza Strip due to security considerations, but we estimate in principle that their number is between 200 and 250... We have many prisoners of different nationalities, and we hope that they will not lose their lives in the barbaric Israeli bombing,' Obeida added, stressing that the foreigners are the resistance's 'guests'... [he] added that at least 22 captives have already died as a result of the bombing of Gaza.[118]*

At the same time, Hamas released a video showing a hostage, Mia Schem, who had been injured and had had surgery in a Gazan hospital. The following day, *The Wall Street Journal* reported that Hamas was prepared to release the hostages.[119] *Aljazeera* reported on October 21 that according to Hamas, Israel had refused to receive two hostages.

> *'We informed our Qatari brothers yesterday evening that we would be releasing Nourit Yitshaq and Yokhefed Lifshitz for humanitarian reasons and without expecting anything in return. However, the Israeli occupation government refused to accept them,' Obeida said on Telegram on Saturday.[120]*

It is difficult to determine the veracity of the accusations and counter-accusations. In fact, Nourit Yitshaq and Yokhefed Lifshitz were released on October 24, and Yokhefed turned to shake hands with a Hamas guard and said "Shalom" (peace).

Revenge, anger, frustration, or deliberate policy?

Adam Shatz, editor of the *London Review of Books* in the United States, wrote an article on November 2, 2023, "*Vengeful Pathologies*".[121] Shatz acknowledges some of the military objectives of the Hamas attack, but they seem to fade when he goes on to assess Hamas's intentions and motives. He seems to suggest that if Hamas had limited itself to military targets, the world's reaction would not have been so strongly opposed. His article could be boiled down to the argument that both parties are equally bad, equally brutal, and vindictive. Palestinians and Israelis are doomed to live alongside each other. Because he doesn't develop this, the tragic conclusion is that since nothing will ever change, the Palestinians must resign themselves to their fate.

Abdaljawad Omar, a PhD student at Birzeit University in the occupied West Bank, responded in *Mondoweiss*[122] under the heading "*Hopeful pathologies in the war for Palestine: a reply to Adam Shatz*". He points out that the predictable, slightly schizophrenic thoughts expressed by Shatz can be understood because he, like many other Western intellectuals, observes the conflict from a comfortable distance and with middle-class disgust for violence, leading him to blame the Palestinians for the spread of fascism in Europe.

> *But the glaring contradiction in Shatz's essay is obvious, yet he seems blind to it: you can see it when he starts his essay by identifying the political objectives of the Palestinian offensive, but then diminishes them to mere 'vengeful' pathologies. He dismisses specific historical analogies, such as the Tet Offensive in Vietnam, without explaining his rationale other than his aversion to violence. These observations are incongruous; either Palestinians had political objectives and indeed opened up a political space that had*

*been shut for years, or they are irrational and barbaric actors driven by an
overwhelming surge of emotion [...]*

*In fact, a prominent emerging perspective is that Israel's reputation as a
calculated, rational, and competent strategic actor is facing severe scrutiny.
The country is fighting to rebuild its image and is becoming increasingly
reliant on NATO assets and power [...]*

*As of now, it appears that Israel has not identified any specific goal other
than 'revenge.' Blinken's visit a few days ago confirmed as much when the
U.S. Secretary realized that Netanyahu has no exit strategy. Finally, why
wouldn't an assault on Israel's primary nerve — its deterrence and military
power — not lead to open new avenues for a new political solution? While
such prospects seem distant in the heat of battle and in light of Israel's genocidal intent, the actual battle on the ground is what will decide the future.
Shatz is particularly unconvincing here, since he already chooses to fore-
close possibilities that might emerge from the aftermath of October 7.*

*By skirting their political utility and military logic and confining them to
mere 'vengeance,' Shatz ignores the fact that all wars and battles, no matter
how horrific, bloody, and tragic, might ultimately create the space for new
possibilities — even hopeful ones. He remains faithful to a dystopian interpretation, providing a darker undertone to the futurity of Palestine and the
world. Perhaps he is right in this and ultimately, all will be losers [...but]
even if the Palestinian resistance fails to snatch a relative victory in this
battle, the alternative would have been a slow death.*

The Pressure Cooker theory

Another theory is the pressure cooker: You can't lock people up in a prison
or a concentration camp for 17 years and expect them to resign themselves to
their fate. There is, of course, a lot to it, and it is probably what explains what
former Israeli Prime Minister Bennet calls "the third wave". But this is hardly
what drives Hamas, who must have been preparing for months for the attack.
Recruiting and training people, acquiring materials, starting the production of
different types of ammunition, extensive intelligence work on the IDF's organization (especially its communication system and the number of troops and
procedures), digging tunnels, distributing materials and people, setting up its
own communication system, etc. And all this time, keeping calm, not allowing
itself to be provoked. And not least, developing smuggling methods to circumvent the blockade.

Gaza and Hamas

The war between Israel and neighbouring countries ended in 1949 with the international recognition of Israel's control over 78% of the territory of the Mandate of Palestine (historical Palestine) with the Green Line as the border – a departure from the Partition Plan the UN had approved in November 1947, which gave the Jewish state 55%.

The 'Gaza Strip' was created at the end of the 1948 war. Israeli forces forcibly transferred hundreds of thousands of Palestinians from the city of Jaffa and districts south of it down to the city of Bir-Saba (now Be'er Sheva) to what became 'The Gaza Strip'. Others were expelled to the Gaza Strip from cities like Majdal (Ashkelon) as late as 1950, in the final phase of ethnic cleansing. A small idyllic part of Palestine was thus transformed into the world's largest refugee camp.[123]

The Gaza Strip was under the so-called all-Palestinian government under Egyptian protection until 1956, with Palestinian passports for its inhabitants. During the 1956 Suez War, Gaza was occupied by Israel, but after international pressure it withdrew, and Gaza was occupied by Egypt. The West Bank and East Jerusalem were then under the administration of Jordan. During the 1967 Six-Day War, Gaza was re-occupied by Israel, as well as the West Bank and East Jerusalem, and now it seemed to be permanent.

Palestinians in exile founded al-Fatah (Arafat's party), heavily influenced by nationalism, socialism, and liberation ideologies of the 1960s (including Cuba, Vietnam, Algeria). The PLO grouped Fatah and other smaller organizations – many of which grew within the Christian Palestinian community – but the movement was distinctly secular. After their victory in the Six-Day War, Israel allowed local elections in the West Bank, and to its dismay, it was the PLO candidates who won. To counter the PLO and other leftist forces, Israel supported the Islamic Society founded in 1979 by Ahmed Yassin, a visually impaired religious leader. The Islamic Society established its own network of schools, clinics, libraries, kindergartens, and even a university, and carried out social work in the occupied territories. Disappointed by the failure of parties inspired by secular and "modern" ideologies to improve living conditions, people turned to religion, searching for comfort and social support. Another group, Islamic Jihad, had taken up arms, and with the first intifada in the 1980s, Islamic Society understood the need for political action. Eventually, in 1988, it was transformed into Hamas, an acronym for the Arab name Islamic Resistance Movement. The disappointment following the failure of the Oslo Accords, which would have resulted in a Palestinian state in 1998, and Ariel Sharon's provocations, led to the Second Intifada when Hamas staged a wave of suicide attacks. Israel assassinated Hamas leaders al-Yassin and al-Rantissi in 2004 but continued its policy of divide and rule.

After 9-11, "Muslim" and "Islam" became, in the West, synonymous with the words terror, violence, inhuman, irrational, backward. In the Western media, Hamas is presented as a sister organization to ISIS, which is wrong – there have been armed confrontations between them. Hamas's aim is the liberation of Palestine and it does not have any international "plan" (ISIS main strategy seems to have been to provoke the West to cause a reaction against it in the Muslim world). The US classified Hamas as a terrorist organization in 1997 and the EU followed in 2003 – Norway and Switzerland maintain contacts with Hamas. Hamas surprised everyone when it ran in local elections in 2005, winning over a third of all municipalities. The following year, Hamas won the election for the Palestine Legislative Council – an exemplary election according to many international observers. It was a shock for Israel and the West who could not understand that fanatical Muslims could be popular and win democratic elections, according to Israeli historian Ilan Pappé.

Inspired, supported, and armed by Israel and the US, the PLO under Mahmoud Abbas tried to manoeuvre against the elected Hamas government leading to a violent conflict. Hamas took control of Gaza and the PLO kept the West Bank. In the West, it was presented as if Hamas had staged a coup d'état in Gaza, but in fact it was the PLO that tried to circumvent the election results through the creation of a separate force under the Presidency. Israel, with US and EU support, blockaded Gaza. Israel applied a "mowing the grass" policy: repeated attacks to keep Hamas in check (see below).

Ariel Sharon, who was Prime Minister between 2001 and 2006, enforced the withdrawal of the settlements in Gaza. It was a masterful move that achieved several objectives:

- The 8,000 settlers who occupied 30% of Gaza (while 1,8 million Palestinians resided in the remaining 70%) were vulnerable to attacks by the Palestinian resistance, requiring significant military and financial resources.

- Sharon allowed the settler movement to incite the settlers in Gaza (who said the evacuation was a new Holocaust) which led to violent confrontations when the police had to carry away some of the settlers. Sharon (known as "Arik the king" by his admirers and "the butcher" by other) managed to appear to Israel and the world as a friend of peace who stood up to fanatical settlers.

- It became easier to control Hamas. It was difficult for Israel to conduct military operations in Gaza when the settlers were there. It could now bomb and attack at will without the risk of reprisals against the settlers.

- Moreover, he hoped to make 1,8 million Palestinians "disappear" from the demographic balance, then ensuring a comfortable Jewish majority in "the country of Israel". Gaza became a no-man's land. Sharon thought that Gaza could be cut off from Israel. Gaza was there but Israel did not engage with Gaza more than punishing its inhabitants regularly. Nobody wanted to know about it, nobody wanted it. Moreover, the Gaza Strip (less than 2% of the British Mandate of Palestine) does not have the same historical significance for the Jews as the West Bank (which they call Samaria and Judea). By withdrawing settlements from Gaza (and some smaller ones in the West Bank), it was possible to concentrate efforts on consolidating the large colonization projects in the West Bank (Ariel, South Hebron Hills), and above all to cut the West Bank in half from Jerusalem eastwards with the big settlement Maale Adumin and Area E1.[124] Israel has always been obsessed with demography and to preserve a Jewish majority, but the Palestinians have a higher birth rate than the Jews, and this constantly threatens the balance. Today there are roughly equal numbers of Jews and Palestinians in the area controlled by Israel – historic Palestine between the Jordan River and the Mediterranean Sea. Israel's wet dream is for the Palestinians to disappear. After October 7, the dream of continuing and intensifying the ethnic cleansing of Palestine was revived with the plan to expel the Gazans to Sinai or even further afield. (Some people have "formulated" conspiracy theories that Israel was responsible of the October 7 attack, so the country had an excuse to expel the Gazans in a new phase of massive displacement of Palestinians, which is akin to state that the 9-11 attacks were the work of the CIA.)

- The ideological confusion was reinforced as Israel, the US, and the EU presented the Palestinian Authority and the PLO in the West Bank as the reasonable side of the Palestinians. The equation became:

    Gaza = Hamas = terror = violence = Islamic fanatics
    West Bank = (relatively) tame Palestinians (who we can control)

The Israeli government continued with its policy of divide and rule. Netanyahu led Israel in several attacks on Gaza while advocating reconciliation with Hamas, a position he justified in 2019 at a meeting with Likud members of the Knesset:

> *In March 2019, Netanyahu told his Likud colleagues: 'Anyone who wants to thwart the establishment of a Palestinian state has to support bolstering Hamas and transferring money to Hamas … This is part of our strategy – to isolate the Palestinians in Gaza from the Palestinians in the West Bank'.*[125]

In the West Bank, the Palestinian Authority (PA) has become increasingly an administrator of the occupation in the hands of Israel, which arbitrarily punishes it by withholding tax payments. The most questionable aspect of the PA is the security cooperation with Israel. The PA is made responsible for "no tolerance of terrorism" which means controlling the population. According to Oslo, the PA is responsible for the security in Area A (the bigger Palestinian towns), but the IDF enters at will to arrest, raid, kill, or simply intimidate. The IDF notifies the Palestinian liaison officer, and the Palestinian police withdraw so the IDF is free to do as it pleases. There has long been strong public opinion questioning the PA in the West Bank, seen by many as a collaborator with the occupation. This has intensified since October 7.

The Israeli government has moved steadily to the right. The current government, installed in the fall of 2022, is the most radical Israel has ever seen – Itamar Ben-Gvir, Minister of Security, and Bezalel Smotrich, Minister of Finance, are openly racist and encourage settlers in the West Bank to violently attack Palestinians. 2023 was the most violent year in a long time for Palestinians. Between January and September 2023, settlers and the IDF killed 234 people, including 45 children in the West Bank.[126] In March, settlers attacked the Palestinian village of Hawwara in what the IDF described as a pogrom, prompting strong international reaction.

Since October 7, violence has increased, resulting in hundreds of deaths in the West Bank. The violence has targeted the thousands of Palestinian prisoners in Israel's prisons. On December 9, 2023, *Haaretz* reported that six Palestinian prisoners had died in Israeli jails since October 7[127] – to cite just one example: 25-year-old Arafat Hamdan was arrested on October 22 in Ramallah, and two days later he was dead. Several prisoners released during the ceasefire at the end of November had wounds and bruises from their imprisonment.[128] It is difficult to obtain precise and verified information, but Israel is holding more than 7,000 Palestinians, many of them in "administrative detention", including several hundred minors. In violation of the Geneva Convention (§76), they are being held within Israel's borders. Palestinians from the occupied territories are brought before military courts, where almost 100% of cases result in a conviction. Palestinians who are citizens of Israel have also been imprisoned after October 7, in Haifa and other cities.[129] Any attempt by Israeli Palestinians to show solidarity with the people of Gaza has been violently suppressed. With the increasingly open crisis within the Israeli government, there have been more anti-war demonstrations, not least demanding a prisoner exchange for the release of hostages. Interestingly, sometimes both Jews and non-Jews demonstrate together.

Palestinians and Israelis killed and injured as a result of the conflict since 2008

West Bank	2008-01-01 to 2023-10-06	2023-10-07 – 2024-01-17	
killed	1,332	359	
wounded	90,342	> 4,325	42 % from tear gas
Gaza			
killed	5,365	*	
wounded	62,998	*	38 % from tear gas
Gaza, not counting the major conflicts (2008/9, 2012, 2014, 2021)			
killed	1,300		
wounded	43,210		
Israel			
killed	319	2008-01-24 to 2024-01-15	
wounded	6 419	2008-01-06 to 2024-01-18	

Between 2009 and 2023, over 16,000 Palestinians have been displaced in the West Bank due to the demolition of their homes and almost 650,000 have been affected by demolitions. In 2023, over 12,600 Palestinians in the West Bank have been affected by the demolition of their houses or other buildings by the IDF (899 cases of demolitions). In East Jerusalem, the figure is 663 people affected by 14 demolitions.
Source OCHA, United Nations Organization for Humanitarian Affairs (https://www.ochaopt.org/).
* Figures for Israel's war on Gaza after October 7, 2023, have not been included, as they are increased significantly daily.

The number of Palestinians working in Israel has been greatly reduced, but there are still several thousand – most in construction and unskilled jobs. Human Rights Watch reported[130] that 3,000 workers from Gaza who were on October 7 were detained and held in isolation for weeks – they were released in early November. They recounted unspeakable atrocities:

> [The Israeli forces] *'made us undress,' he said. '[We were] completely naked. They handed us Pampers to wear and thin white overalls.... We stayed blindfolded and cuffed [with zip ties on our hands and feet] for 10 days... We kept asking why we are detained. We never got an answer, only verbal assaults and death threats.'*

On October 7, 2023, Israel's dreams of displacing larger numbers of Palestinians were reawakened. After decades of denying that any Nakba had taken place – it was even forbidden to publicly acknowledge it in Israel – Israeli ministers, politicians, and leaders say that what must be done in Gaza is a new Nakba:[131] "We are now rolling out the Gaza Nakba" said Israel Agriculture Minister Avi Dichter. Can Israel do this? It is not impossible, but it requires more than will and power on Israel's part to make it happen. It must crush Hamas, which most observers believe is very difficult; and in addition, other countries must be prepared to tolerate it, and accept 2,3 million refugees. And, not least, the Palestinians must agree to it, voluntarily or by force.

Since the blockade of Gaza in 2007, Israel has carried out regular military campaigns, "mowing the grass" with the aim of limiting Hamas's ability to attack Israel – occasional rockets fired by Hamas could be tolerated but Israeli bombing and ground invasions were expected to keep Hamas in check. A similar policy was implemented in southern Lebanon to limit Hezbollah military capabilities. The major operations against Gaza are in chronological order:

May 2004: Operation Rainbow

2006: Summer Rain

September 2007: Locked Preschool

2008–2009 war: Cast Lead – 1,417 people were killed in Gaza, the overwhelming majority of them civilians, including nearly 300 children and 103 women. Thirteen Israelis died.

2010: Operation Sea Breeze against Ship to Gaza.

2014: Protective Edge. OCHA (United Nations Organization for Humanitarian Affairs) reported 2,220 Palestinians killed, of whom 1,492 were civilians (551 children and 299 women), 605 "militants". Israel reported 64 dead.

In Gaza, there is a *no-go zone* inside the barrier. Israeli forces have largely restricted access to areas within 300 metres of the Gaza side of the outer fence with Israel; areas several hundred metres beyond this are not considered safe, preventing or discouraging agricultural activities according to the UN. This means about 5% of Gaza's territory is a no-go zone and that the *risk zone* – which the UN estimates to be up to 1,000 metres wide – is equal to up to 15% of Gaza's area. Moreover, Israel has repeatedly reduced the area that Gaza's fishermen are allowed to use. It is now only 50% of the fishing waters set aside for this purpose under the Oslo Agreement. Israel has long used calculations to determine how much food can enter Gaza to avoid a famine but keep Hamas in check.[132]

Let us mention just a few points from the report issued by the UN on the tenth anniversary of Israel's continued blockade of Gaza:[133]

> *Following Hamas' violent take-over of Gaza in June 2007, stringent restrictions in the form of a land, air and sea blockade were imposed. In terms of imports, only 'basic humanitarian products' (primarily food, fodder, medical supplies, and hygiene items) were allowed in. A complete ban on exports and transfers of goods to the West Bank during the first two years of the blockade led to the closure of 95% of Gaza's industrial establishment and the loss of 120,000 jobs. Palestinian access to farming land and fishing areas was also significantly reduced at this time as more than 76,000 dunams of land [7,6 km²] along the fence line were categorized as 'Access Restricted Areas' (ARA) and fishing grounds were also reduced by at least half by the Israeli navy. During this phase, restrictions on the exit of Palestinians through the Erez crossing was limited to 'humanitarian cases', and three of the four crossings for goods between Gaza and Israel were shut down. The impact of the closures was further aggravated by the near complete closure of the Rafah crossing by Egypt during the same period, and smuggling tunnels under the border with Egypt became the main point of entry for construction material, livestock, fuel, cash and food products.*

The entire Palestinian economy in the Gaza Strip, West Bank and East Jerusalem, is a *captive economy*,[134] totally dependent on Israel – not only because the currency used is the Israeli shekel, but because Israel controls all entry and exit of goods, services, transport, and currency. Under the rules of the Oslo Accords, it is Israel that collects taxes, including on imports and exports and the funds are to be transferred to the Palestinian Authority. Israel has systematically used these funds to pressure both the Palestinian Authority in Ramallah and Hamas in Gaza.

Gaza's economy has *under*developed.

Most businesses in Gaza are traditionally family owned and operated and are largely engaged in trade and services. Businesses are usually small, with the majority employing only 1–4 people. Gaza businesses fare much worse than their counterparts in East Jerusalem and the West Bank... Gaza's private sector is the engine of any future economic growth but remains severely constrained by the restrictions on movement and access to natural resources and markets, in addition to the recurrent destructive outbreaks of hostilities. With an economy in free fall, 70 percent youth unemployment, widely contaminated drinking water and a collapsed health system, Gaza has become unliveable... all parties – especially Israel – [must act to] end this disaster.

The War in Gaza

Speaking to his commanders after the three hostages were killed by their own people on December 15, 2023, Israel's commander-in-chief General Herzi Halevi stated three goals for the war: crush Hamas, re-establish the security of the Gaza Envelope, and free the hostages.

Israeli journalist Yuval Abraham writes: "Contrary to initial claims, the Israeli army carried out relentless strikes with little intelligence of Israeli hostages' whereabouts or precaution for their safety, a +972 and Local Call investigation shows".[135] His source, who wished to remain anonymous,

> emphasized that the army 'would not have killed hostages deliberately if they knew they were in a certain building,' but that it nonetheless carried out thousands of strikes knowing full well that hostages might be also harmed, especially at a time when 'there were many hostages held in private apartments' [above ground]
>
> … Noam Dan [some of her family members were kidnapped in Gaza]… 'When the hostages were released, we realized that many of them were above ground, in people's homes. The government kept telling us that they knew where they were, that they wouldn't do anything that would endanger them, that everything was under control. But once the abductees got out of there, these things turned out to be false. Everything we thought [was true] collapsed.' [...]
>
> Dan added that, from conversations she had with freed hostages, she learned that their primary fear was being killed or wounded by the Israeli army's attacks — a feeling echoed by other captives released in recent weeks. She also said that there was evidence of hostages being hit by Israel's bombing in Gaza… One source explained that… there was a sense that 'the lives of the hostages were a price that people in the army, especially senior commanders, were willing to pay'.

There has been much speculation that Netanyahu's political life, as well as the army leadership's, is over, and therefore they must continue the war as long as possible in the hope of somehow managing to present some result resembling a victory.

The Soldiers' Conduct

Some films on the internet are creating problems and eroding Israeli self-confidence. In December 2023, several videos of uncomfortable incidents were published, presumably filmed by the soldiers themselves. One of them shows soldiers smashing toys in a toy store; in another they take items from private homes.[136] A video from December 8 shows Israeli troops setting fire to objects in what they say is a candy factory in the Gaza Strip. The soldiers joke that the fire represents "the second light of Hanukkah". It is forbidden to deliberately destroy property in war. However, the most shocking is a video where a soldier shows a necklace and jokes in front of the camera: "Look, he bought you a necklace, 'Made in Gaza', it has a love heart. Woah! It's a necklace: forever." He shows it to the other soldiers, then bites it and says, "Let's see if it's real!"[137]

The images of scores of half-naked Palestinian men sitting and being guarded by armed soldiers are also shocking and can hardly be reconciled with respect for prisoners and are reminiscent of other wars.

Eran Halperin, a professor at Hebrew University told the *Los Angeles Times* that

When people feel they were humiliated, hurting the source of this humiliation doesn't feel as morally problematic. When people feel like their individual and collective existence is under threat, they don't have the mental capacity to empathize or apply the moral rulings when thinking about the enemy.

The problem and scale of abuse has only increased. The Aljazeera podcast The Listening Post's episode "The unravelling of the New York Times 'Hamas rape' story" (see note 85), refers mainly to the suppression of free speech in Western countries but it is worth viewing from the 14th minute:

… in one video after another, Israeli soldiers have recorded their own war crimes, celebrating as they looted homes, destroyed houses, or set them on fire; filming as they mocked, humiliated, and assaulted Palestinian captives. It is a sign of the impunity they think they have […]

Palestinians have seen this kind of thing before, going back to 1948. But never have the images, the videos been this widespread, explicit, and barbaric. The Listening Post has collected some of that material and asked three experts on Human Rights and Torture to assess it. First a view warning: many of the images in this report are difficult to take in.

The on-screen text reads: "*All of the material in this report was filmed by Israeli soldiers in the occupied Gaza Strip. Soldiers shared the material on social media platforms. The Listening Post collected and reviewed more than 250 photos and videos over the course of four months.*"

The journalist warn that it is hard to take in. It is indeed. Try it yourself.

Human Shields

One brilliant commentator has said that every accusation made by Israel against the Palestinians is in fact an admission. One of the most common arguments to justify civilian casualties is that Hamas uses human shields and that the IDF is fighting a war under unique circumstances.

The Israeli organization *B'tselem* writes:

> "Israel says Hamas is to blame for these figures because it uses civilians as human shields, conceals weapons in their homes, and fires at civilian targets in Israel from within a civilian population, allegedly leaving Israel with no choice but to harm civilians in its war against Hamas. According to this view, assigning full responsibility to Hamas means that every action taken by Israel, however horrific the outcome, would be considered legitimate. Such a claim is baseless. Respect for the law, international humanitarian law included, is not subject to reciprocity: failure by one side to comply does not give the other license to do the same.[138]

The argument that the war in Gaza is unique has no basis. The circumstances in the war against Hamas resembles numerous larger or smaller wars in the past and nowadays – in Vietnam, Algeria, and several other countries, urban and rural guerrillas have faced a superior regular army. During the German occupation of European countries in World War II, resistance movements fought in a similar way, as did the Jewish militias in Palestine in their war against the British. Avi Shlaim, Professor of International Relations at Oxford University, born in Iraq, who calls himself an "Arab Jew", writes in a forthcoming book on the war in Gaza that "having been denied the fruits of its electoral victory, Hamas resorted to the weapon of the weak, to what Israel calls terrorism…".[139] This has been a fundamental condition of many wars of liberation and resistance movements against an occupying army – as Mao put it: "The people's army must move amongst the people as a fish swims in the sea".

Israel reverses the rhetoric, but in fact the settlements in the West Bank and the so-called Gaza Envelope are human shields. Israel claims it has troops in the West Bank and between the kibbutzim and communities around Gaza to protect civilians, but the reverse is equally true. If Israel cared about its civilians, it would not have moved 700,000 of its citizens to live among the Palestinians in the West Bank, knowing that this is where "terrorist organizations" are born and grow. In order to entice its citizens to expose themselves to this risk, the state offers various benefits, including financial incentives for settlers.

The communities of the Gaza Envelope were granted the status of Confrontation-line Communities in 2013 and given special privileges. No less than 54 communities and kibbutzim are included in the Gaza Envelope. The very name – Gaza Envelope – suggests that it is a military strategy. In other words, civilians are used to achieve a military objective.

It is important to note that from the earliest stages of the yishuv (Jewish settlement in Palestine) a century ago, the rural kibbutzim were as much agricultural communities as military posts. This is hardly unique, but mostly a condition of any establishment in a hostile environment. In this case, however, the environment was not hostile from the start. But the new colonists had a long-term, aggressive plan and realized that sooner or later their neighbours would understand and resist, as Ze'ev Jabotinsky expressed in *The Iron Wall*:

> *There can be no voluntary agreement between us and the Palestine Arabs. Not now, nor in the prospective future… Zionist colonization… can proceed and develop only under the protection of a power that is independent of the native population – behind an iron wall, which the native population cannot breach.*[140]

The Likud party program (see Appendix II) states that "settlements in all parts of the Land of Israel are of national importance and part of Israel's defence strategy. The government will allocate special resources for settlement in border and sparsely populated areas." In other words, the population on the ground, especially in border areas such as the Gaza Envelope, is part of the defence strategy.

After the October 7 attack, there were numerous statements from the Israeli president on down through the ranks like, "there are no innocents in Gaza", they are "human animals", and similar expressions. Major General Eitan Dangot, an advisor to three Israeli defence ministers, told *i24NEWS* on October 10, 2023:

> *We have come to the end… because we lost the safety and security that we have to provide to civilians living around Gaza… there is no distinction between Hamas in Gaza and civilians in Gaza; the word humanitarian policy will no longer be used, we have to cut off water, cut off electricity, all supplies, cut off everything… we will not show them any compassion, no obligations, no things that the laws prescribe …*

On October 10, 2023, Israeli Defence Minister Yoav Gallant said, "I have lifted all restrictions; we have taken control of the sector and are moving to a full-scale attack. Hamas wanted a change in Gaza; we will make a 180-degree turn towards what they want."

It could be argued that some of this was a result of rage, of speaking in anger. General Dangot is not a government spokesperson, but what he said was exactly what was done: cutting off electricity and water and all supplies, including fuel, eventually leaving hospitals without electricity, lifting all restrictions, no mercy. Such statements were later repeated. As recently as December 20, 2023, Neftali Bennet, former Israeli Prime Minister, was interviewed by the *BBC*. He began by saying, "we don't attack civilians", but later he said:

Let me tell you what the civilian population of Gaza felt on October 7th before Israel struck back. The lion's share of Gazans massively supported Hamas... [It is] very unfortunate that we are dealing with a population that thinks that it is good to rape women and murder children if they are Jews. If I could choose another neighbour I would... but we need a new regime [in Gaza], one that stops brainwashing the children.

As an explanation of the killing of the three hostages who managed to escape from Hamas only to be killed by the IDF, Bennet said that "the soldiers have been away from their families for a long time, have barely eaten... mistakes are being made".

When the journalist confronted him with the fact that health services in Gaza have been completely obliterated – 364 attacks on health facilities, 553 people killed inside hospitals, and 729 wounded, Bennet replied: "Every school, every hospital is a base for terrorism".

Bennet claims that one cannot compare the two sides. But is this true? An overwhelming majority of Israelis support the occupation, directly or indirectly – all governments in Israel since 1967 have expanded the settlements – 700,000 Jews, about 10% of Israel's Jewish population, live in settlements in occupied territory. Does this make these Israeli civilians legitimate targets? The same is true in most wars. The majority of British, Soviet, and German citizens supported their countries' war efforts. Were they legitimate targets? Did Hitler have the right to bomb Coventry, besiege Leningrad; did the Allies have the right to bomb Dresden or the United States to nuke Hiroshima and Nagasaki when the war was practically already won? Of course not.

The fact that Gazans or Palestinians in general support Hamas does not mean they are combatants, just as not all Israelis are combatants. The Geneva

Conventions say nothing about what views or sympathies Protected Persons may or may not have.

This is nothing new. During the 2014 war on Gaza, "Protective Edge", Amira Haas, a journalist at *Haaretz*, wrote an article entitled "How many civilians is a militant worth?"

It is perhaps superfluous to say more about the distinction between civilian and military targets when even the US has talked about indiscriminate bombing by Israel in Gaza. But Nefatli Bennet's dismissal of *B'tselem's* criticism is interesting: "They are self-hating Jews".

B'tselem allows anyone who opens their website (January 23, 2024) to read a single headline in huge white letters on a red background: "Israel is starving Gaza", where we read:

The 2.2 million inhabitants of Gaza are hungry. This is not a by-product of war but a direct result of Israel's stated policy. The population is now completely dependent on food from outside because stocks in Gaza have run out and there is almost no way to produce food. Israel is deliberately not letting enough supplies into Gaza and refuses to change this policy despite the growing risk of famine. Starving a civilian population and blocking humanitarian aid is considered a war crime.

Human Rights Watch wrote on December 18, 2023: "Israel: Starvation Used as Weapon of War in Gaza – Evidence Indicates Civilians Deliberately Denied Access to Food, Water."[141]

Reports claim that Israel has consistently allowed the entry of the food calculated as 2300 calories per person – sufficient to avoid a famine disaster but keeping the population in an iron grip, always at the limit, in order to put pressure on the Hamas government in Gaza.[142]

There is a video on the IDF website[143] showing a soldier opening a machine in a hospital and taking out a gun in a plastic bag. It is impossible to verify whether it is authentic or a constructed scene. If it is true, it is a war crime. But… a pistol in a war zone? Does it prove that Hamas used the incubators as weapons or that the IDF wants to convince the world that it has the right to "obliterate the health sector" (as the WHO put it)?

Children in incubators at al-Shifa hospital had to be evacuated to Egypt when Israel occupied the hospital, and six died on the way. At al-Nasr hospital, where Israel forced an evacuation, five premature babies were found dead in incubators, their bodies having begun to decompose, *The Washington Post* reported.[144] A whole book could be written just on attacks on health services in Gaza: dead doctors and other staff, dead patients, imprisoned and missing health workers, attacks on ambulances. This is nothing new either. If you search the internet, you will find numerous stories of babies born at roadblocks in the West Bank. Between 2000 and 2005, 67 women were forced to give birth at Israeli roadblocks in the occupied West Bank. Thirty-six of the babies, more than half, died.[145]

After many days inside the hospitals in Gaza, the IDF has failed to produce any evidence to support its claims that hospitals have been used as "terrorist bases", *The Washington Post* wrote on December 21, 2023:

"… a Washington Post analysis of open-source visuals, satellite imagery and all of the publicly released IDF materials. That raises critical questions, legal and humanitarian experts say, about whether the civilian harm caused by Israel's military operations against the hospital — encircling, besieging and ultimately raiding the facility and the tunnel beneath it — were proportionate to the assessed threat.

The Post's analysis shows:

- The rooms connected to the tunnel network discovered by IDF troops showed no immediate evidence of military use by Hamas.

- None of the five hospital buildings identified by Hagari appeared to be connected to the tunnel network.

- There is no evidence that the tunnels could be accessed from inside hospital wards.[146]

It seems quite reasonable to agree with Ghassan Abu-Sittah, a British-Palestinian surgeon who spent 43 days amidst the Israeli offensive on Gaza performing 10 to 12 surgeries per day, and who was witness to the targeting of civilians when he says that the systematic destruction of the health sector is one of the means whereby genocidal war and ethnic cleansing is being waged on Gaza.[147]

What does Israel want?

Despite the fact that many commentators have claimed that "Hamas aimed to kill as many civilians as possible" (because they are Jews, according to Neftali Bennett) and that the comparison with the Holocaust was made immediately, not least by senior US officials, we have seen that it is far from clear how many of the victims who died on October 7, civilians as well as soldiers, either fell to Hamas bullets in battle, were killed by Hamas men or Gazan civilians, fell in crossfire, or were killed by Israeli bombs and missiles from helicopters, airplanes, and tanks.

Israel entered the war with full force and has rejected almost all proposals for negotiations, except for the brief pause at the end of November to exchange captured women and children. The Israeli government and the IDF have consistently stated that the goal is to eradicate Hamas, which is supported by violent rhetoric and propaganda that several jurists and international organizations call "genocidal". Proving intent is one of the most difficult aspects of proving the claim of genocide, but in this case, it is clear from statements that all Gazan civilians are considered guilty, Gazans are animals, etc.

Cartoons have appeared on the internet that would be the envy of Nazi hate propagandists, according to Natasha Roth-Rowland, a PhD student of the history of Israel and Palestine, under the title, "When never again becomes a battle cry: the anti-Semitic propaganda of the 1930s". On the Israeli news site *+972magazine*,[148] she writes:

> *Indeed, the constant invocation of the Holocaust seems to have done little to sensitize those calling for Gaza's destruction to [the Holocaust's] lessons. In addition to the demands for vengeful mass killings and the abundant references to Palestinians as 'animals', Nazi-like imagery has also been making the rounds among hasbarists [Israeli propagandists] on social media; in one drawing that could have come straight out of Der Stürmer [a Nazi propaganda magazine], an IDF boot is pictured about to step on a cockroach with the head of a Hamas fighter...*
>
> *The irony is transparent and grotesque: the very kind of obscene propaganda that helped fuel unimaginable atrocities is being adopted to, ostensibly, ward off a repetition of that same history — and to justify ongoing ethnic mass killing and collective punishment...*
>
> *This 'Holocaustization' of what is happening in Israel-Palestine deposits all of us — Jews, Palestinians, those in the region and in the diaspora — on*

a dangerous precipice. To operate within that framework, according to its internal logic, is to condemn us to a zero-sum war whose terms are clear and devastating: a conflict that can only ever be resolved by the annihilation of one side or the other. It is a recipe for perpetual bloodshed — an exhortation, in the words of Netanyahu, to 'live forever by the sword.'

The IDF and the Israeli government seem driven by other forces as well. Wounded pride and humiliation after Hamas succeeded in paralyzing the army, revenge, and hatred. There was a huge contrast at the November 2023 prisoner exchange between what happened in Gaza, where the Red Cross and Hamas cooperated in a dignified transfer of the prisoners, and the ravaged faces of the Palestinian prisoners released from Israeli jails, some with obvious signs of abuse.

Where does this hatred come from? The Israeli leadership must know they are lying. The military leadership knows that planes, helicopters, and tanks killed many of their own people, but cannot, at least not yet, admit it. Israel behaves as if it is above everything and everyone. As Craig Mokhiber, the head of the office of the UN High Commissioner for Human Rights in New York, said, there are special rules when it comes to Israel, an exceptionalism: Israel is unique. So it is, in many ways.

Israel is the only country created by a UN decision – General Assembly Resolution 181, the Partition Plan for Palestine. It is paradoxical that Israel has the record of ignoring UN decisions and can get away with no consequences whatsoever. So, the legal basis for the existence of the State of Israel is the Partition Plan,[149] but that is not how Israel sees it. Both before and after the proclamation of the state on May 14, 1948, the Zionist leaders were clear about this. The Partition Plan was for them a tool, not what gives the state of Israel the right to exist. Menachem Begin wrote in the *Irgun* newspaper during the UN discussions on the Partition Plan:

> *The division of our homeland is illegal. We will never recognize it. Signing the Partition Plan has no value. It will never apply to the Jewish people. Jerusalem was and will always be our capital. Eretz Israel will be returned to the people of Israel. All of it. And forever.[150]*

David Ben Gurion, the first Prime Minister of Israel, was an atheist. A very famous statement of his reads:

> If I were an Arab leader, I would never sign an agreement with Israel. It is normal; we have taken their country. It is true God promised it to us, but how could that interest them? Our God is not theirs…

(Ben Gurion was not telling the truth here, the god of the Muslims is the same as that of the Jews – Mohammed's revolution was to throw away all the idols from the Kaaba and return to the true god, the god of Abraham).

The Bible is a great literary work, not a history book, especially not the books of Moses, which collect several legends and myths from all over the region, especially from Persia.[151] But the Bible is central to Israel's self-image. Zionism – the political branch of Judaism that claims Palestine should be colonized by the Jews – describes the conquest of Palestine as a return, not a conquest. According to a 2014 Israeli Ministry of Education circular to all schools, "the Bible constitutes the cultural infrastructure of the State of Israel and in it the right to our land is anchored."[152]

The ruling Likud party's party platform states:

a) The right of the Jewish people to the Land of Israel is eternal and unquestionable and is tied to the right to security and peace; therefore, Judea and Samaria [i.e., the West Bank] will not be handed over to any foreign administration; between the sea and the Jordan River there will be only Israeli sovereignty.

b) A plan which cedes parts of Western Eretz Israel undermines our right to the land, leads inevitably to the establishment of a 'Palestinian state', jeopardizes the security of the Jewish population, endangers the existence of the State of Israel and destroys all prospects for peace.[153]

The text does not mention the Bible but provides another very relevant piece of information. "Western Eretz Israel" is nothing more than the area currently controlled by Israel – the British Mandate, the historic Palestine, the area between the Jordan River and the Mediterranean Sea. If there is a Western Eretz Israel one can guess there is an Eastern Eretz Israel. In fact, some Zionists also claim that Jordan and parts of Syria, Lebanon, and Egypt belong to the Jewish people. From time to time, some lunatic comes along claiming that Israel must occupy "all of Eretz Israel", but for somehow realistic politicians this is just an illusion, a dream – at least for the time being. What is abundantly clear is that the State of Israel does not consider itself bound by the UN Partition Plan, which it accepted because it knew that the Palestinians and neighbouring countries would never accept it, and which it never intended to respect.

Curiously, in 1949 the UN agreed to recognize "facts on the ground", abandoning one of the most central principles of the UN: states must not conquer territory by force or threat of force. The UN recognized that in the 1948–1949 war with the Arab countries, Israel appropriated more territory than the Partition Plan intended. The partition plan had stipulated that 55% would go to the Jewish state and 45% to the Arab state. But Israel occupied 78%, the area within the 'green line', a fact that was accepted by the UN – a precedent that Israel learned important lessons from. It believed – rightly, as it turned out – that it could do whatever it wanted. The only exception has been the Suez War in 1956 when Israel, France, and Britain attacked Egypt after Nasser nationalized the canal and the US said 'no' – according to Vice President Richard Nixon, the US could not oppose the Soviet invasion of Hungary while approving Israel's invasion of Egypt. From then on, however, Israel did as it pleased – taking the Golan Heights from Syria and the Sinai from Egypt (which was returned when Israel and Egypt established diplomatic relations a few years after the 1973 war), invading Lebanon several times, and claiming the right to bomb neighbouring countries whenever it wants. There are numerous examples that prove that Israel – when it comes down to it – does not feel bound by any international laws. Israel conducts covert operations in all countries as if it had the right to do so. (It has gotten into trouble because of this – in some cases because it used foreign passports for its secret agents – but was later forgiven).

The question is why the world has tolerated Israel acting like a bully?

"Israel is a Democracy"

It is often claimed that Israel is the only democracy in the Middle East. This is not true – for example, Jordan is internationally recognized as a democracy. But what about Israel's oft-cited democracy? Adam Shatz, editor of the *London Review of Books* in the US, quoted a Palestinian Knesset member: "Israel is democratic towards Jews, and Jewish towards Arabs".

The vast majority of scholars call Israel an ethnocracy, not a democracy. British historian Toni Judt argued that Israel was an anachronism, that the era of colonial policy based on a religious myth is past; Israel might have worked 300 years ago, but not now.

> *In spite of Israel's success to advertise its regime as such, it is often defined by researchers as either an 'ethnocracy' (Yiftachel 2006) or as an 'ethnic democracy' (Smooha 1997). This is because ethnicity and not citizenship is the main determinant for the allocation of rights, power and resources in Israel.*[154]

Here we will discuss two questions: is Israel an apartheid state or a democracy? And does the legal system work?

There was a lot of excitement when the UN Economic and Social Commission for Western Asia published the report "Israeli Practices towards the Palestinian People and the Question of Apartheid"[155] on March 15, 2017. The newly appointed UN Secretary-General Antonio Guterres demanded that the report be withdrawn, but Rima Khalaf, the head of the Commission, refused and resigned two days later. The report was written by Virginia Q. Tilley, Southern Illinois University Carbondale, and Richard Falk, an American lawyer who was the UN Special Rapporteur for the Palestinian Occupied Territories between 2008 and 2014. Israel has long been referred to as an apartheid state in activist circles, such as the BDS movement. When I was in Israel in 2011, people involved in civil organizations in Israel acknowledged that the country was an apartheid state, but it was impossible for them to say so publicly. The President of South African, Nelson Mandela, and Archbishop of Cape Town, Desmond Tutu, compared the situation in Palestine with apartheid South Africa (Israel was the last country in the world to persist in supporting the apartheid regime in South Africa after the EU and the US had washed their hands of it). Although the UN withdrew the report, it had a huge impact. The wording "Israeli apartheid" began to be uttered in contexts where it had not previously been possible. In January 2021, the Israeli human rights organization *B'tselem* (The Israeli Information Centre for Human Rights in the Occupied Territories) explained its position on the issue:[156]

> *Roughly 15 million people, about half of them Jews and the other half Palestinians, live between the Jordan River and the Mediterranean Sea, under a single rule. The perception that there are two separate regimes in this territory – a democracy on one side of the Green Line, within Israel's sovereign borders, and a temporary military occupation on the other – is divorced from reality.*
>
> *All of us, Jews and Palestinians alike, live in this area in a binational reality, under a single regime. However, not everyone will be permitted to vote in the coming elections, which will determine the government and our lives in the coming years. About half of the population – all the Palestinians who live in this area, whether they are citizens, permanent residents or subjects – are either fully or partially excluded from this decision-making process.*
>
> *One regime governs the entire area and the fate of everyone in it. This regime operates according to a single organizing principle: advancing and cementing the supremacy of one group – Jews – over another – Palestinians. Under this regime, Jewish citizens have the monopoly on political power. Only they have a true seat at the table where their fate, and the fate of Palestinians, is determined.*
>
> *This is not a democracy. This is apartheid.*

A few months later, Human Rights Watch published the report "A Threshold Crossed – Israeli Authorities and the Crimes of Apartheid and Persecution", and in February 2022, Amnesty International headlined a report: "Israel's apartheid against Palestinians: Cruel system of domination and a crime against humanity". From then on it was widely accepted that Israel is a regime of apartheid in spite of Israel and its defenders persisting in calling the country a democracy.

Further down in this section is a list showing how different groups in Israel are treated differently under Israeli law, which is the very essence of apartheid. There are no less than thirteen different groups. It is not possible to delve into the myriad of procedures that Israel uses to make life difficult for Palestinians, in the hope that at least some of them will give up and leave their land – in addition to the arbitrary violence, which kills and maims people and even imprisons children, simply to, as many former Israeli soldiers tell in the book

Breaking the Silence,[157] "instil fear in the Palestinian population". Breaking the Silence describes itself as

> *an organization of veteran soldiers who have served in the Israeli military since the start of the Second Intifada and have taken on the task of showing the public what everyday life is like in the Occupied Territories. We seek to stimulate public debate on the price paid for a reality where young soldiers encounter a civilian population on a daily basis and are solely responsible for controlling their daily lives. Our work aims to end the occupation.*[158]

A small example[159] can illustrate how the occupation works like a well-oiled machine to make life sour for Palestinians: A young man who owns a small shop in Hebron went to buy a few cartons of ice cream that would last a while. He was hurrying back, it was midday and the sun was warming up. He had to pass a roadblock. The soldiers, young men and women his age, decided to examine the packages. He protested but it couldn't be helped. The soldiers opened the boxes and spread the packages over a large table and forbade the man to approach: "We have to go through everything". It takes time, a lot of time. The man becomes more and more desperate. "This is our life!" he shouts as he realizes that there is no way to save the ice cream.

No blood, no loud noises, no shooting. Just a quiet drama, a slow, soft violence that penetrates people's lives. So devastating is the "bureaucratic terrorism" that Palestinians live under in the West Bank, in addition to other forms of more overt violence, such as night raids, beatings, destruction of property, house demolitions, attacks by settlers, fighting to try to protect their animals, or being imprisoned themselves – today maybe the farmer just takes a few blows from the settlers and a few hours in jail; maybe he, the victim, has to pay a fine, maybe not. "This is our life!"

> *The fundamental difference between South African and Israeli colonialism is that the former wanted both land and people while the latter wants only the land.*[160]

In May 2017, Knesset Deputy Speaker Bezalel Smotrich (now Finance Minister) announced his "Israel's Decisive Plan".[161] The aim was "to erase all Palestinian national hope". According to the plan, Palestinians will be offered three choices: to leave the country; to live in Israel as a "resident alien" since "according to Jewish law there must always be some inferiority"; or to resist – "the Israel Defence Forces will know what to do". When asked if he meant wiping out entire families, including women and children, Smotrich replied: "In war, as in war."

Israel has a judicial system with courts of various levels and the Supreme Court at the top. The system works. Palestinians in the occupied territories are subject to strict military laws and are brought before military courts to convey the appearance of legality. There is some possibility to appeal, and the process can end up in the Supreme Court, which sometimes rules in favour of the little guy. However, in May 2016, the human rights organization *B'tselem* said that it no longer considered litigation worthwhile. The military legal system is a fig leaf, *B'tselem* explained in the report "The Occupation's Fig Leaf: Israel's Military Law Enforcement System as a Whitewash Mechanism".[162]

The village of Kfar Birim in northern Galilee, near the border with Lebanon, was occupied by Zionist militias on October 31, 1948, just like more than 530 other Palestinian villages in 1948 and 1949. The militias drove the inhabitants away, saying that it was only for the duration of the unrest, then they would be allowed to come back. The Melkite priest, later archbishop, Elias Chacour's family was from the village, and he tells in his book *We belong to this Land* (University of Notre Dame Press, 2000) about the villagers' struggle to return to their community and farm their land, which amounted to almost 100 hectares. When the war was over, they tried to return but were prevented by the military. They started litigation and got as far as the Supreme Court, which ruled that the residents had the right to return to Birim. But before they could, the village was flattened by Israeli aircraft, which also destroyed their farmland, on September 16, 1953.

Different groups, different rights and opportunities

Within the areas under Israeli control between the Jordan River and the Mediterranean Sea, there are different groups of citizens with different legal, economic, and social rights and opportunities.

1) Jewish citizens of Israel living within the Green Line (the internationally recognized border). In theory, everyone has the same rights, but there are several sub-groups depending on origin and skin color. It is very difficult for those not belonging to the *Ashkenazi* (European Jews) elite to reach high positions in the state apparatus and military leadership. Historically, there have been abuses against "non-white" groups – most famously, children of Yemeni, Ethiopian, and Oriental Jews were taken from their mothers and put up for

adoption by white families.[163] Jews studying in religious schools (Yeshiva) are exempt from military service.

2) Palestinians who are citizens of Israel (about 20% of the population, 1,8 million) have, in a formal sense, most of the rights that Jews have, with some exceptions. The kibbutzim, many rural communities, and urban residential areas may be closed to them as these define themselves as Jewish Only communities. Land in Israel is managed by the Israel Land Administration which restricts in various ways the right to own and cultivate land for non-Jews. Most Palestinians live in communities that receive step-motherly treatment from the state, less funding for municipal projects and services, less police coverage. In addition, many communities are not allowed to expand because they are not allowed to acquire more land, increasing overcrowding and social problems. Some government services are not available to Palestinians who are citizens of Israel because they are exempt from military service, which is a requirement for some positions.

Early on, the Absentees' Property Laws were passed to expropriate all property belonging to people who were not within the country's borders, i.e., 80% of Palestinians, who had been expelled from what is now Israel to neighbouring countries. Some Palestinians were refugees within the borders of the State of Israel, like the inhabitants of Birim. They became citizens of the country but were prevented by the state from settling on their property. They were called Present Absentees, and their property was also confiscated. Palestinians who remained within the borders of the State of Israel, were, between 1948 and 1964, subject to military laws, not the ordinary civil law which governed Jewish citizens.

3) Bedouins in the Negev living in "unrecognized communities". Only communities that are recognized by the state receive public services such as water, electricity, schools, etc. Many Bedouin villages have never been recognized, which means that they are not allowed to build permanent buildings (if they do, the police come and demolish them); they receive no water, no electricity, no schools, etc. Most live in tents. For example, one of these villages, Al-Araqib, has been demolished by the police more than a hundred times, but each time it is rebuilt.[164]

The state has long-standing plans to have the Bedouins settle in specific areas or communities. Community planning is openly based on ethnicity and on securing the Jewish majority.[165] The state pursues plans for the Judaization of various areas such as the Galilee, the Negev, and East Jerusalem.[166]

4) Palestinians living in East Jerusalem. They are not Israeli citizens, although Israel has annexed East Jerusalem – a decision that is illegal under international law. They have a permanent residence permit for East Jerusalem. They can live in Jerusalem but not in other parts of the country. The residence permit can be reconsidered at any time for various reasons. If you go abroad to study or for other reasons spend a long time outside the country, you may lose your right to live in Jerusalem. Municipal services in Palestinian areas are often inadequate and the contrast with the fine Jewish Only settlements is striking. They are also threatened by a stricter interpretation of legislation. It is almost impossible for them to obtain building permits, leading to overcrowding. Israeli authorities can at any time require them to prove that their "Centre of Life" (an interpretation of where you belong) is in East Jerusalem. If the authorities consider that one's Centre of Life through their job or other reason is not Jerusalem, they lose their resident permit. If one chooses to marry a Palestinian living in the West Bank or elsewhere, they are not allowed to settle in Jerusalem. There are couples who live apart and only see each other occasionally. A war of attrition is taking place in East Jerusalem as individuals and groups of Jews claim, with the help of Israeli lawyers, that they are entitled to a particular house or an entire neighbourhood. Sheik Jarrah[167] and Silwan[168] are two such areas where Jewish settlers are constantly advancing their positions, with the aim of taking over areas and displacing their inhabitants.

5) Jews living in settlements in East Jerusalem have the same rights as group 1.

6) Jews living in settlements recognized by the Israeli government in the West Bank enjoy the same rights as group 1 but have some economic benefits. Many of the men in these settlements form a regular paramilitary force. They carry heavy weapons, guard their areas, and attack Palestinians. A subgroup is those living in the H2 area of Hebron. They are not numerous but very militant. The entire city centre has been turned into a ghost town because of them.

7) "Youth of the Hills" are often young families who settle in – according to the State of Israel – illegal outposts established on land often privately owned by Palestinians. They usually start with a few caravans and then build houses and eventually receive electricity and other services from the state, in addition

to protection from the military, even though these settlements are illegal under Israeli law. Most of them are very militant and dangerous to the Palestinians living around them.

8) Palestinians in the West Bank, who in turn are divided into several sub-groups after the Oslo Accords:

8.1) Residents in A zones where the Palestinian Authority has full responsibility for civil affairs (schools, health, building permits, and community planning, etc.) and for security. The latter, however, is a truth with modification; the IDF comes as often as it pleases and arrests people, raids, searches, kills, shoots, throws tear gas grenades, etc. Area A includes the main Palestinian cities in the West Bank: Jericho, Ramallah, Tulkarem, Qalqilya, Salfit, Yatta, Nablus, Bethlehem, Jenin, Tubas, and part of Hebron.

8.2) Palestinians living in B Zones, where the Palestinian Authority is responsible for civilian affairs while responsibility for security is in the hands of the IDF. Those living in these areas have their land at their disposal, but sometimes cannot access it because it is on the other side of the wall or because the IDF has closed the roads. They are regularly subjected to attacks, arson, destruction of crops and trees, killing of livestock. But perhaps more significant is the "bureaucratic terrorism": through an endless number of laws and regulations issued by the military, their lives and freedom of movement are controlled, and they are subjected to all kinds of harassment and restrictions in their lives in matters large and small. These communities and smaller towns are heavily affected – even during "quiet" periods – by the nearly 700 roadblocks in the West Bank that cause delays and humiliation. Most medium-sized communities are located within B zones.

8.3) Palestinians in Area C (60% of the West Bank) which is entirely under IDF control. It is virtually impossible to obtain building permits. Residents have difficulties using public services and their freedom of movement is severely restricted. A particularly vulnerable group are those living in the Jordan Valley.

8.4) The Bedouins in the desert area east of Jerusalem, who live under similar – but more precarious – conditions than the Bedouins in the Negev Desert.

8.5) Hebron is a divided city. Palestinians rule in area H1, but the IDF in area H2 which includes what was once the city centre, where Palestinian residents live under strict restrictions; some, for example, have to enter their houses through the roof, because the street entrance is sealed. The streets are empty and there are special corridors for Palestinians living there. Here, residents are subject to constant harassment by the settlers.

9) Palestinians in Gaza, the largest open-air prison in the world.

Not to mention the Palestinian refugees in the neighbouring countries.

Nurit Peled is a researcher at Hebrew University in Jerusalem. She has long researched schooling in Israel, and in particular how textbooks present Palestinians, Arabs, and Jewish minorities (Ethiopian, Yemenite, Oriental Jews – *Mizrahim*, the Jews who lived in the Middle East among the Arabs), who are called "ethnicities":[169]

> *both non-Jewish 'minorities' and Jewish 'ethnicities' are represented, both verbally and visually, in a racist manner, as stereotypes and not as individuals. Palestinian citizens and those who live under a military regime in the Palestinian occupied territories are presented – if at all – as vile, primitive, and dangerous. Jewish 'ethnicities', which include mainly Arab-Jews and Ethiopian Jews, are represented in an 'anthropological' way, mostly as under-developed 'sector' … The Palestinian territories are presented as part of Israel and yet the inhabitants of these same territories are foreigners. However, the readers may not be aware of this peculiarity because the occupied territories are not marked as Palestinian areas. Both groups are culturally and socially marginalized in textbooks as they are marginalized in Israeli society. The multimodal analysis allows a unified perception of this representation, which reveals ideological undertones and interests.*
>
> *This stands in contradiction to the persistent Israeli claim, echoed by American and European politicians who endorse Israeli policy, that "Palestinians teach their children to hate us and we teach Love thy Neighbour". As this paper demonstrates, one of the aims of the Israeli-Zionist narrative, which can be seen in each phase of the Zionist project, is to create a homogenous 'Western' identity for all the Jewish 'ethnicities' in Israel. This identity requires the rejection and denial of all other identities, languages and religious practices, and acceptance of the Israeli Hebrew ones.*

Underlying all this is the goal that Zionism has always had, which can be summarized in a single sentence:

as much land as possible with as few people as possible.

Zionism was founded in the 19th century on the myth that Palestine was a land without a people and the Jews a people without a land. Neither was true, as Ilan Pappé explains in his book *Ten Myths about Israel.* In order to obtain land without a people, between 1947 and 1949, the Zionist militias expelled more than 80% of the native population of the areas that became the State of Israel. They were expelled through force or fled after being terrorized by massacres such as those in Tantura, Deir Yassin, and other Palestinian towns and villages – this is what the Palestinians call the Nakba (catastrophe). Some 530 villages and towns were emptied of their population and many of them razed to the ground.

In the 1980s, the state began to open its archives and a group of historians, Benny Morris, Ilan Pappé, Avi Shlaim, Simha Faplan, and others began to question some of Israel's myths, such as that the Palestinians had left their villages voluntarily. They showed convincingly that the Jewish militias had expelled them, that there had been outright ethnic cleansing.[170, 171]

Recently, more documents began to emerge about the 1947–1949 war against the Palestinians.

> *Testimonies continue to pile up, documents are revealed, and gradually a broader picture emerges of the acts of murder committed by Israeli troops during the War of Independence. Minutes recorded during cabinet meetings in 1948 leave no room for doubt: Israel's leaders knew in real time about the blood-drenched events that accompanied the conquest of the Arab villages,*

wrote Adam Raz on December 9, 2021, in *Haaretz:*[172]

> *It was November 1948. Testimonies of massacres perpetrated by IDF soldiers against Arabs – targeting unarmed men as well as elderly folk and women and children – were piling up on the cabinet table. For years these discussions were concealed from the public by the military censors. Now, an investigative report by Haaretz and the Akevot Institute for Israeli-Palestinian Conflict Research for the first time makes public the sharp exchanges between the ministers on this subject and reveals testimonies about three previously unknown massacres, as well as new details about the killing in Hula, Lebanon, one of the most flagrant crimes of the war.*

The long article describes abuses in Reineh, near Nazareth, Al-Burj, today's Modi'in, Meron, Saliha, Safsaf, Al-Dawayima and other villages. It is a horrifying read about murders, mass executions of men, women, children, old people, looting, rape.

For these crimes, just one person was sentenced to one year in prison. The judges explained that the lenient sentence was because he was the only one put on trial while others who had committed more serious crimes were not prosecuted. He was pardoned and later became general director of the Jewish Agency. A "code of silence" prevailed among the soldiers.

In Safsaf (today Moshav Safsufa), near Safed, soldiers from the 7th Brigade massacred dozens of inhabitants. According to one testimony (subsequently reclassified by the Malmab unit), 'Fifty-two men were caught, tied to one another, dug a pit and shot them. Ten were still twitching. Women came, begged for mercy. Found bodies of 6 elderly men. There were 61 bodies. 3 cases of rape.'

In the village of Al-Dawayima (today Moshav Amatzia), in the Lachish District, troops of the 8th Brigade massacred about 100 people. A soldier who witnessed the events described to Mapam officials what happened: 'There was no battle and no resistance. The first conquerors killed 80 to 100 Arab men, women, and children. The children were killed by smashing their skulls with sticks. There wasn't a house without people killed in it.' According to an intelligence officer who was posted to the village two days later, the number of those killed stood at 120.

An article published by an anonymous soldier in the journal Ner after the war indicates that the phenomenon of killing non-combatants was widespread in the IDF. The writer related how his comrades in the unit had murdered an elderly Arab woman who remained behind during the conquest of the village of Lubiya, in Lower Galilee: 'This became a fashion. And when I complained to the battalion commander about what was going on, and asked him to put a stop to the rampage, which has no military justification, he shrugged his shoulders and said that 'there is no order from above' to prevent it. Since then the battalion just descended further down the slope. Its military achievements continued, but on the other hand the atrocities multiplied.'

'This is a Jewish question.'

In November-December 1948, when the war pressure had abated somewhat, the government turned to discussing the reports of massacres, which reached ministers in different ways. A perusal of the minutes of these meetings leaves no room for doubt: The country's top leaders knew in real time about the blood-drenched events that accompanied the conquest of the Arab villages. ...

Even those who did not have the benefit of silence and a cover-up, and were tried for crimes committed in the war, were finally let off the hook. In February 1949 a retroactive general pardon was issued for any crimes committed during the war. The public at large appears not to have been disturbed by any of this. The events described above took place during the period when the military justice system was being created. This might explain why the military internalized an organizational culture that goes easy on the killing of Palestinians by soldiers during operations. The philosopher Martin Buber termed the frame of mind that dominated Jewish society at the time a 'war psychosis'.

*Half a year later, the first Speaker of the Knesset, Joseph Sprinzak, appeared before the parliament's Foreign Affairs and Defence Committee. Mentioned in the meeting were two items that had appeared in the press that day, which epitomized the attitude towards the acts of murder during the war. One report referred to an officer who during the fighting had ordered the murder of four wounded individuals; the second report was about a person who sold stolen army equipment. The former was sentenced to six months in prison, the latter to three years. Sprinzak, in any event, was under no illusions. **'We are far from humanism', he told the committee. 'We are like all the nations'.***

Ofer Aderet, wrote in *Haaretz* on January 5, 2022:[173]

Minister's remarks in 1948 that he can 'forgive instances of rape' and Ben-Gurion's assertion that some Palestinian villages must be 'wiped out' were censored from unclassified docs, but exposed due to technical error ...

It turns out that Israel's first agriculture minister, Aharon Zisling, who was a signatory to the Declaration of Independence, said in 1948 that he 'can forgive instances of rape' committed by Jews against Arab women. Seventy-four years have gone by since then, but the State Archive still believes that the public must not know this. Here is the entire statement:

'Let us say that instances of rape occurred in Ramle. I can forgive instances of rape, but I will not forgive other acts'. The next statement, which was not blacked out, now gains additional significance, and explains what the minister considered an act more serious than rape: 'When they enter a city and forcibly remove jewellery from women and from their necks – that is a very serious matter'.

"Israel has the right to defend itself"

Does Israel have the right to defend itself? The question is not as simple as one would like to make out.

It can be argued that Israel, like all states, has the right and duty to defend its population. But in the case of Israel, there is another equally strong duty. As an Occupying Power according to the Geneva Convention, Israel has the duty to protect the civilian population in the occupied territories and provide for their needs.

The starting point must therefore be that Israel has been violating international law for a long time and is deliberately sabotaging it by not complying with mandatory UN resolutions. The UN and the international community regard East Jerusalem, Gaza, the West Bank, and the Golan Heights as occupied territories. Which in itself is a very strange thing to consider. An occupation is meant to be temporary, until the conflict can be resolved. But Israel has skilled lawyers working on ways to get around this. According to Security Council Decision 242 adopted in November 1967, Israel is obliged to leave the occupied territories, but has not done so and certainly does not intend to do so, as is (and always has been) clearly stated in the program of Likud, the main governing party (most other Israeli politicians might not write it so clearly, but that's how they think) and demonstrated in the books of Simha Flapan, Ilan Pappé, Avi Shlaim, Benny Morris, and others.

According to the Geneva Convention, the occupying power has, in principle, the same obligations as any other government towards the civilian population of the occupied territories, who are Protected Persons. They are to be protected, guaranteed work, income, social services, not be imprisoned without reason, etc. There are two main limitations: one –the occupying power can, if military necessity so requires, restrict access to an area; two – it is forbidden to make major changes to the landscape and social structure of the occupied territory, including moving its own population to the occupied territory. The question is whether Israel is entitled to defend itself in this specific context – that Israel's occupation has been illegal for more than 50 years, that Israel has violated almost every single article of the Geneva Convention, that Israel does not treat the civilian population of the occupied territories in accordance with the Convention, as Protected Persons, but as enemies.

To argue that Israel has the right to bomb occupied territories is like saying that the British had the right to bomb Northern Ireland in the 1960s and 1970s.

If Israel wants to ensure the safety of its population, the solution is quite simple: end the occupation, withdraw all troops, discontinue the settlement, start negotiations under Resolution 242 to solve the question of the Palestinian refugees.

The preamble to the Universal Declaration of Human Rights states: "Whereas it is essential, if man is not to be compelled to have recourse, as a last resort, to rebellion against tyranny and oppression, that human rights should be protected by the rule of law".

It does not take long to realize that Israel's occupation violates many of the rights of the Palestinians and that they are thus in the situation expressed in the Universal Declaration: "compelled to have recourse, as a last resort, to rebellion against tyranny and oppression". So, the question is not whether Israel has the right to defend itself but whether the Palestinians have the right to revolt against "tyranny and oppression".

There are already too many "facts on the ground", realities that must be taken into account. Ariel Sharon said, when he was Minister of Agriculture: "We will turn the West Bank into a salami. It will be impossible to talk about an Arab state there." He meant filling the West Bank with settlements. He succeeded.

Ehud Barak, the Israeli politician who perhaps came closest to resolving the conflict, described Israel as a "villa in the jungle". Josep Borrell, the EU's foreign policy chief, recently said "Europe is a garden… The rest of the world is not exactly a garden. Most of the rest of the world is a jungle, and the jungle could invade the garden."[174] Is there an invisible line between these statements and Israel's insistence on comparing the Palestinians to the Nazis? Owen Jones, who saw the IDF's propaganda film for the war in Westminster, argues that any comparison between Palestinians and Nazis diminishes the crimes of the Nazis and is insulting to the victims of Nazism.

But the Israeli Major General Eitan Dangot argues that: "…you can't compare with the Holocaust, these are animals…"[175] A remarkable statement from a man whose father was a Holocaust survivor; he seems to imply that the Nazis were somehow better than the Palestinians.

References to the Holocaust, when the Nazis murdered six million Jews, are legion in this context. Gideon Levy, a journalist for *Haaretz*, explained in 2015[176] what

> *enable[s] us Israelis to live so easily with this brutal reality [the occupation of Palestine]. A) If not all, most Israelis are deeply convinced that we are the chosen people. And if we are the chosen people, we have the right to do what*

we want. B) There have been more brutal occupations in history. There were even longer occupations in history, although the Israeli occupation has a pretty good record. But there has never been an occupation in history where the occupier portrayed himself as the victim... We say victims, we say chosen people. When I say victims, it is obvious that we have to mention the Holocaust and the unforgettable Golda Meir that American Jewry had exported to Israel. She once said – this unforgettable woman – that after the Holocaust the Jews have the right to do what they want.[177]

Almost everything in Israel is linked to the Holocaust. Israeli Foreign Minister, Abba Eban, considered the greatest "dove" in Israeli politics, coined the phrase "Auschwitz borders" for Israel's 1949 armistice lines. Even today, writes Avram Burg, they are still called that. "Israel must never return to the pre-war borders".[178] Burg cannot be accused of being a pro-Palestinian propagandist – he is a devout Jew, was Speaker of the Knesset between 1999 and 2003, and Chairman of the Jewish Agency. His book *The Holocaust is Over and We Must Rise from the Ashes* is a 260-page argument that Israelis must rid themselves of Hitler and the Holocaust:

Israel's security policy, the fears and paranoia, feelings of guilt and belonging are products of the Shoah [The Holocaust]. Jews-Arab, religious-secular, Sephardi-Ashkenazi relations are also within the realm of the Shoah. Sixty years after his suicide in Berlin, Hitler's hand still touches us ... indeed we have force, a lot of force and only force. We have no alternative to force, no special notion or will to hold back our use of force.[179]

This is not a rhetorical figure. He continues:

What keeps this country together are the wars. Often we say that we are lucky to have the Arab as our enemy, otherwise we would have devoured one another long ago."[180]

The Shoah is our life, and we will not forget it and will not let anyone forget us. We have pulled the Shoah out of its historic context and turned it into an excuse and the motivation for every deed. All is compared to the Shoah, dwarfed by the Shoah, and therefore all is allowed – be it fences, sieges, extrajudicial executions, curfews, food and water deprivation. All is permitted because we have gone through the Shoah, and you will not tell us how to behave. Everything seems threatening to us.[181]

Moshe Sharett, Israel's first foreign minister and later prime minister, wrote in his diary on May 26, 1955:[182]

> *Dayan's argument was as follows... In reality, we face no military threat whatsoever from the Arab states... On the other hand, retaliatory actions are vital to us... Without these actions, we would cease to be a fighting nation, the colonizers would begin to leave the settlements. We must tell these colonizers that the US and Britain want to take the Negev from us. It is essential to convince our young people that they are in danger. The implications of Dayan's words are clear: this state has no international obligations – there can be no peace. Israel must live by the sword and chart its course by conspiracy. It must see the sword as the primary and only means of maintaining its morality. To this end it can – no, it must – invent dangers that do not exist and to do this it must use provocation and revenge tactics. Above all, we must hope for a new war with the Arab states so that we can finally get the space we need. Dayan reminded us that Ben-Gurion himself had said that it would be worth paying an Arab a million pounds to start a war against us.*

Everywhere, this feeling that one does not have to respect any law or the rights of others, that the Holocaust explains everything one wants to do. Ronen Bergman writes in his book about Israel's practice of targeted killings:

> *The Jewish people have been humiliated, trampled, murdered [...] Now was the time to strike back, to take revenge [...] It was that sense of lost honour, of a people's humiliation, as much as rage at the Nazis, that drove men like Gichon. [...]*
>
> *In the years following the war, the Zionists of the Yishuv would prove, both to the world and, more important, to themselves, that Jews would never again go to such slaughter – and that Jewish blood would not come cheaply. The six million would be avenged. ... 'We thought we could not rest until we had exacted blood for blood, death for death,' said Hanoch Bartov.[183]*

But again, why does the world let Israel behave like this? (The world would never have given France, the Soviets, Vietnam, or Iraq the right to take revenge in this way...)

> *The horrors that befell the Jews of Europe during the Hitler era [have] forever absolved Israeli governments of all moral and political responsibility for their actions. Israel must therefore go uncriticized for actions that inter-*

national opinion would never have tolerated if performed by democracies, thereby allowing Israeli governments to place themselves outside the rules of international law.[184]

Hand in hand with the Holocaust is anti-Semitism, which is sometimes portrayed as if it were the only form of racism to be cared about. Everyone knows what anti-Semitism has led to. Nobody wants to promote the trends and ideas that led to the destruction of European Jewry, nobody wants to know about Hitler, nobody wants to be a Nazi. An effective weapon to paralyze enemies and opponents is to accuse them of being anti-Semites. As a reflex, every time someone criticizes Israel, the label anti-Semite is used. In the collective European consciousness, anti-Semitism epitomizes evil itself and is used as a kind of anathema against anyone who dares to criticize Israel. (And if you are a Jew who criticizes Israel, then you are a self-hating Jew, because no Jew can question Israel's right to behave as it wants.)

Accusing the Palestinians of Nazism is historically inaccurate, a complete reversal of roles, but Israel has managed the feat of reincarnating the Nazis in Arab form and the West has swallowed the message. Everything and everyone that threatens or attacks Israel evokes memories of Nazi brutality and therefore it has become an automatic reflex to react without even knowing what has happened. It evokes, on one hand, the unconscious thoughts that have dominated Europe for so many centuries, the colonial fantasies of the "white man's burden", the image of the "other", savage and uncivilized, irrational and violent, represented today by Hamas and the Palestinians in the same way that people talked about Orientals at the time of the Crusades; Africans, Arabs, or indigenous people on the American continent and in Australia; about the slaves in the United States. The colonial fantasies evoked by Ehud Barak as well as Joseph Borrell, resound in the words of Theodor Herzl, the founder of Zionism, who saw the Jewish settler colony in Palestine as "the portion of the rampart of Europe against Asia, an outpost of civilization as opposed to barbarism."[185] There are these unconscious fantasies which Israel's propagandists try to evoke – the brutal, savage rapist – the same fantasies that led to so many lynchings of black boys and men in the US's South, accused of raping white women. Some of the supposed witnesses to sexual violence expressed themselves in a way that is itself suspicious: "I saw this beautiful woman with the face of an angel..."[186] What if she was ugly? Should it be a minor crime?

On the other hand, there is in Europe's elite the conscious or unconscious panic of being reminded of the role, direct or indirect, by complicity, by sympathy, by action or by omission, that many countries played in the accession of the Nazis to the government in Germany and the destruction of European Jewry.

Does Israel then have the right to defend itself?

Certainly, not the right, but the duty, to protect itself, its population, and, according to the Geneva Convention, also the Palestinians. The legitimate defense that Israel should have applied a long time ago would have been to stop ignoring international law and proceed to apply UN General Assembly Resolution 194 to allow the Palestinian refugees to return home, to comply with UN Security Council Resolution 242 of 22 November 1967, retire from East Jerusalem, the West Bank, Gaza, and the Golan Heights, and end the occupation. Is it surprising how much energy the West has put into demanding that Palestinians recognize Israel's 1949 borders and Resolution 242 while at the same time not demanding the same from Israel: to withdraw from the occupied territories. Israel has no plans to leave the West Bank (which it calls Judea and Samaria), Gaza, and least of all East Jerusalem, or the Syrian Golan Heights, or to take any steps to resolve the situation of the Palestinian refugees.

In fact, the solution is simple: forget the nonsense about God's chosen people, leave the master race mentality and behave like normal people.

But instead, Israel brings in Jews from Europe and the US to use them as human shields in settlements, among them extremists who terrorize Palestinian children on their way to school, killing farmers' sheep and burning their crops and trees.

Raz Segal, an Israeli expert on modern genocide, calls Israel's attack on Gaza "a textbook example of intent to commit genocide", and its rationalization of the violence a "shameful use" of the lessons of the Holocaust. The Israeli state exceptionalism and comparisons of its Palestinian victims to 'Nazis' are used to 'justify, rationalize, deny, distort, disavow mass violence against Palestinians,' in what constitutes a 'shameful use' of the lessons of the Holocaust", Segal said in an interview with Amy Goodman on October 16, 2023.[187] A few weeks later, on October 28, Craig Mokhiber, the head of the Office of the UN High Commissioner for Human Rights in New York, resigned and wrote a long letter declaring that the UN was failing in its duty to act against the genocide taking place in Gaza. As early as March 2023, he had written to his superiors about a series of serious violations in the West Bank, including the Hawwara pogrom. He understood that fear was paralyzing the UN and that there was pressure to silence human rights lawyers and experts, "including myself". He then said he would resign in November 2023:

> *The UN and its members have a duty not only to respect but also to act to ensure that international law is respected… Starting with the Oslo process 30 years ago, the UN basically abandoned the old approach of focusing on international law, international human rights, and equality in Israel and Palestine… Now the United States is not only guilty of inaction, but is also complicit by arming and giving diplomatic support to the genocide being carried out by Israel. The international community has rules, but when it comes to Israel, there are other rules. This is frustrating. Where is the UN protection and the Security Council?*

Conclusions: So, what do we really know about what happened on October 7?

Reading this section may give one the impression that the aim is to excuse Hamas. This is not the case, but before condemning Hamas, we need to know what really happened. The truth is that there is a lot of uncertainty about what happened and that even around what is clear, it is not entirely clear who did what.

We know that Hamas[188] started the day by firing a large number of rockets towards southern Israel as well as towards Jerusalem and Tel Aviv. Several Israeli citizens died, and others were injured by the rockets. At the same time, Hamas disrupted the IDF's communication system and destroyed the remote-controlled and automatic weapons that crown the Gaza wall, tore down the wall and fences in more than thirty places, took control of the Erez crossing (the only then-active "entrance" to Gaza from Israel), and crossed the barrier into Israel in paragliders and through the breaches with cars and motorcycles, quickly overrunning several military posts, including the Gaza Division headquarters at Kibbutz Re'im. In some places, Israeli soldiers offered resistance. But by and large, the Palestinians succeeded in paralyzing the IDF in the Gaza area, which was left without leadership and without communications. Hamas took control of several communities and kibbutzim in the so-called Gaza Envelope. In some cases, Hamas maintained control for a couple of days, perhaps until Monday, October 9. Hamas also captured several soldiers and officers and took them to Gaza. Many civilians were taken to Gaza as hostages. Some of those civilians were kidnapped by civilians as video evidence shows, but it is not clear whether Hamas men took civilian hostages to Gaza or not – Hamas has denied this charge and maintained that they only captured soldiers or armed civilians.

There is no doubt that Hamas managed to take over and neutralize all military positions in the Gaza Envelope. But there are few reliable figures for or details about how many Hamas men crossed to the other side, little complete information about which kibbutzim and communities they occupied, when and for how long, and what operations were conducted in cities like Sderot. Among the Gazan civilians who entered southern Israel, there were those who were armed and others who were not. There is no doubt that both Hamas and civilian Gazans killed Israeli civilians, possibly also soldiers who had surrendered, but there is no reliable and verified documentation on the details.

Hamas had no knowledge of the Nova Festival (which was due to end the day before) and it is unclear whether Hamas attacked it or whether it was just Gazan civilians who went there and seized the opportunity to kidnap and kill people. Noah Argamani and her boyfriend Avinathan Or were taken to Gaza by some unarmed youths.

We know that after only a few hours, helicopters arrived whose crews, with no guidance and no communications, initially unsure of what to do, then started shooting at anything that moved, both inside the kibbutzim and in the communities, at the Nova Festival, and in the area around the Gaza barrier where there was a lot of movement. It is not difficult to understand that many people in Gaza got out just because it was possible.

There were 28 helicopters in the air. Airplanes also took part in attacks on some military positions. For example, General Rosenfeld, the head of the Gaza Division, directed the aircraft to bomb his barracks. Both Hamas and the IDF used naval units.

Tanks took part in the fighting at Kibbutz Be'eri and elsewhere. In the festival area, large areas of land were completely scorched, and a large number of cars were demolished and completely burnt out with or without their passengers, suggesting that it was from Hellfire missiles fired from helicopters or fighter jets. This is also what American former diplomat Chas Freeman believes.

There was fighting in Kibbutz Be'eri, Kibbutz Kfar Azza, and elsewhere and many civilians were hit in the crossfire between Palestinians and IDF soldiers or other armed Israelis. The total destruction of houses in Be'eri, Kfar Azza, and other kibbutzim and communities is likely the result of Israeli aerial bombardment or heavy combat-vehicle fire. Hamas could hardly have carried such weapons. Rockets from Gaza could have caused some devastation, but this is not mentioned by journalists or Israeli officials interviewed, who always blame the destruction on Hamas on the ground. Rockets from Gaza killed and wounded people in more remote locations such as Be'er Sheva and Tel Aviv, including several Palestinians.

On January 12, 2024, Ronen Bergman and Yoav Zitun wrote in the Hebrew supplement *7 Days of Yedioth Ahronoth* under the headline "The Black Time". Dena Shunra translated the article for *The Electronic Intifada*, published in full on January 20, 2024, under the headline "Israeli HQ ordered troops to shoot Israeli captives on October 7" (Asa Winstanley[189]). The Israeli journalists Bergman and Zitun have an extensive network of contacts in the Israeli army and security services (Ronen Bergman is the author of the book *Rise and Kill First*). The article deals with the events of October 7. Already the night before, the Israeli high command had an inkling that something was in the making, but no major preparations were made, even though, according to the authors, Israel had had access to Hamas's "Jericho Wall Plan" for a year, which seems to match the October 7 attack to the letter. The article is a detailed account of what happened in the Israeli high command (called "The Pit", an underground control room in Kirya, Tel Aviv) the night before and during October 7, and in the field from 6:26 a.m., when the rocket attacks began, until midday.

From the article, I conclude:

1. *The* Hamas *attack was carefully planned and had the central military objective of taking control of the Gaza Envelope and capturing as many soldiers and officers as possible.* This required:

   a) Disabling the IDF communications system by taking down antennas, towers, observation posts and other installations. The High Command in Tel Aviv had, for several hours, to rely on social media information, especially what was published by Hamas, to know what was happening.

   b) Knocking out the automatic weapons atop the wall and the sophisticated warning systems at the barrier, allowing the creation of more than 30 breaches. The article includes a map with 48 red dots signalling holes in the barrier.

   c) Attacking the Gaza Division headquarters located in Kibbutz Reim and the large number of military posts throughout the Gaza Envelope.

   d) Preventing the arrival of Israeli reinforcements by taking control of the roads and intersections including Gama, Magen, Ein Habesor, and Shaar Hanegev, where they had taken positions with machine guns and anti-tank weapons.

The number of Hamas men who participated is still very unclear. The article estimates that 2,000 men from Hamas's elite Nukhba force invaded Israel through the Erez Crossing and breaches in the barrier. Battles between the IDF and Hamas elite forces occurred in more than 80 locations.

2. The IDF was caught completely off guard, and several air force units (drones, airplanes, and helicopters) were ordered to "fire at will". The drone operators of "Zik" (Elbit Hermes 450) received the following instruction at 07:43: "You have permission to fire at will", meaning: shoot at anything that appears to be a threat or the enemy. The pilots communicated via their phones with acquaintances on the ground and used *WhatsApp* groups to get information because there was no functioning military communication system.

The Airforce was also confused, and the order given (at 08:58) was similar: "Shoot anyone who intrudes in our space, without [waiting for] authorization", squadron commander Lieutenant Colonel A told his subordinates in the air, while he himself took off for the Gaza Envelope. One of the helicopters was damaged by small arms fire but continued fighting.

At 09:30, the commander of a helicopter unit ordered the crews to fire over the entire area, until further notice.

The IDF was using uncalibrated weapons, 20-year-old munitions, and soldiers had no equipment, such as bulletproof vests. "For a few hours we fired in the Gaza Envelope without hitting any terrorists."

Eventually, commanders of the secret command unit *Hupat Esh*, some of whom were only 22 years old, sent the Apache pilots a command that has never appeared in any standing order: "You have permission until further notice – and throughout the entire area."

11:59: Chaos and confusion reigned for many hours. The first video footage of captured soldiers now arrived. "It was at this moment that the IDF decided to revert to a version of the Hannibal directive, without using the word, and despite the IDF's repeated assurances that the directive had been abolished."

The IDF leadership at the time thought it was "a couple of hundred terrorists" when it was perhaps ten times that number. The instruction was to "prevent people from entering Israel and going back to Gaza". At least 70 cars and pickup trucks were bombed, despite their not knowing – then as now – how many captured soldiers and officers or Israeli civilians were in them.

The aircraft bombed many targets where there were Israeli troops as close as a few dozen metres.

In addition to IDF troops, many other Israelis took part in the fighting. The *Shin Bet* ordered all men who had weapons and combat training to go to the area and fight.

3. Through the many breaches in the fence, people poured into Israel (08:32). At one stage, helicopters and drones fired indiscriminately at them to force them back into Gaza. When new breaches were discovered, the same thing happened there. The article talks about tens of thousands of people getting out of Gaza, but it is difficult to know the exact number. In firing to "prevent people from entering Israel and going back to Gaza", many hundreds, perhaps thousands of Gazans were killed.

4. The IDF estimated that Hamas lacked the capacity to launch more than a very limited attack.
   "This is what happens when your enemy knows much more about you than you know about the enemy", write Bergman and Zitun.

When IDF spokesman Daniel Hagari said that Hamas was waiting for the Nova festival visitors with a machine gun, the intention was to mislead. He knew full well that Hamas was waiting with automatic weapons at the crossings to stop military reinforcements – something the IDF would not admit, just as Israel would not admit that many of the Israeli civilians and soldiers killed on October 7 were killed by friendly fire from planes, helicopters, tanks, and drones. The 7 Days article leaves little room for speculation that Hamas's goal was to attack military targets and that they succeeded in this aim, and not to "kill as many civilians as possible", "desecrate and humiliate women" and other claims that Israeli propaganda has incessantly fed to the Western media to explain the widespread scorched earth tactics in Gaza and to cover up the humiliating defeat suffered by the IDF.

In summary, it is unclear:

- how many soldiers fell in combat with Hamas, and how many soldiers were killed by friendly fire during combat or by missiles and shells fired from helicopters, airplanes, and tanks;

- how many Israeli civilians were killed by Hamas, by Gazan civilians, in crossfire, or by IDF missiles and shells fired from helicopters, planes, and tanks;

- how many Hamas men made it to the Gaza Envelope and came back and how many died, and under what circumstances, in combat or from missiles and shells fired from helicopters, planes, and tanks, or also from friendly fire;

- whether Hamas took civilian hostages to Gaza and whether Hamas took the bodies of dead Israelis to Gaza, as the IDF claims (this may be a way of trying to excuse the killing of hostages during the bombings of Gaza);

- how many Palestinian civilians made it across to Israel, how many of them were armed and not, how many took part in actions against Israelis, took hostages, killed or injured people, and how many of these were killed, when, where, and how.

What is clear is that it is incorrect to say that "Hamas killed 1200 persons on October 7, most of them civilians". But we cannot put accurate figures to the following statement: "Hamas killed … people on October 7; … soldiers and … civilians. Gazan civilians killed … people. During the IDF's counterattack, … people were killed, … of them civilians, and … soldiers. In the crossfire, … civilians and … soldiers died".

The Hannibal directive was clearly applied during October 7 and the days following. Israeli aircraft and armoured vehicles killed several people, including Israelis. Mark Regev's admission that 200 completely burned bodies thought to be Israelis but which turned out to be Palestinians is evidence of the great confusion on October 7 and that the IDF is responsible for an unknown but probably large percentage of the Israeli dead. The completely burnt bodies in a car presented by the IDF can only be explained by the fact that a missile hit the car and the occupants died instantly – soft body parts and car interior completely incinerated by the blast.

Judging by the sheer scale of the devastation at the festival site, with cars demolished and large areas of scorched land, it appears that a significant part of the deaths were caused by attacks from the air, i.e., by Israeli attack helicopters or fighter jets. How else does one explain the large areas of scorched land and the many destroyed cars? We know that the IDF attacked kibbutzim and communities with tanks and that helicopters fired missiles at them.

We may never know, but it cannot be ruled out that a significant number of the Israeli civilians killed were victims of missiles and shells fired from planes and tanks, and crossfire inside the communities. The admission by Yoav Zitun in *Yedioth Ahronoth* on December 12, 2023, that it was deemed "not morally sound to investigate" how many died by friendly fire because of "the enormous and complex number of these cases that took place on the kibbutzim and in Israeli communities in the south as a result of the challenging situations in which the soldiers found themselves", demonstrates a deliberate attempt to bury the truth (which is what the article he wrote with Ronen Bergman in *7 Days* is, in part, revealing).

What would the consequences be for the State of Israel and the IDF if it turned out that 10 or 20 percent or even more of the Israelis who died were killed by the IDF – victims of helicopter missiles and tank shells, and that October 7 was a far worse failure than the 2002 hostage crisis in Moscow's Dubrovka theatre where 15% of the hostages died during the Russian police's rescue operation?

We also know that some senior officers in the IDF and the Israeli government headed by Prime Minister Netanyahu and President Herzog systematically lied and fed the media and public opinion with false information. The 40 beheaded babies is only the most grotesque example.

The story of beheaded babies may have originated with Colonel Golan Vach or General Barak Hiram who claimed to have found eight burnt babies, or a mother and her beheaded baby. None of this was true. Prime Minister Netanyahu then increased the number to 40, adding together the burned and beheaded. So, the ball was rolling: 40 burned and beheaded babies. Israeli statistics show that in reality one baby was killed on October 7 – which is tragic enough.

Many people claim to have heard or seen the "terrorists" say and do things that are hard to believe, partly because of the circumstances, but mainly because they are contradicted by more reasonable testimonies – such as those from Kibbutz Be'eri. It is possible that many of them believe what they say, but many stories, especially those from the shelters next to bus stops and of sexual abuse, seem to be constructed and shifted from one witness to another, then repeated by one newspaper and quoted by the next and then taken up by supposedly serious people creating the impression of a serious verification when nothing of this exists.

The major campaign on sexual violence (which still continues) was also a failure when *The New York Times*' article on December 28, 2023, "Screaming Without Words: How Hamas Used Sexual Violence as a Weapon on October 7", turned out not to be true. Gal's sisters and brother-in-law denied the claim that she had been raped and accused *The New York Times* of deceiving and exploiting the family. Within *The Times* staff now fear a new scandal like "The Caliphate".[190]

A common feature is that allegations are launched with big headlines, generalities, lots of adjectives and lots of emotion but little effort to gather circumstantial evidence or do proper research. The media – as well as most Western politicians and leaders – has failed in its investigative and source-critical task by allowing Israeli propaganda-trained officers or spokespersons to speak, without commenting critically, or by simply taking one side's statements at face value (the Israeli side). As if they had never heard that the first casualty of war is the truth.

But the propaganda, campaigns, and headlines will continue. The dough will be baked and baked again, a new headline will be found, and it will be cranked round and round. It has an effect. Repeat something often enough and people will eventually believe it. Use the emotions. That's how propaganda works. This is what the media should see through, but they fail.

The reasons given by Israeli officials and civil women's groups for not having evidence of rape (and the use of hospitals as military bases, and many other things) are many: there was no time, there was confusion, bodies must be buried as soon as possible because the religion requires it – notwithstanding that the IDF's Chief Rabbi said on October 13, 2023, that

> *a considerable number of the fallen soldiers are not easily identifiable, and their identification requires the use of advances technology. This process is lengthy, and it takes a considerable amount of time. Precision precedes speed. With the large number of casualties, it is imperative to ensure that each soldier is identified beyond a shadow of doubt.*

Most remarkably, Israel's spokesperson on sexual abuse, Cochav Elkayam-Levy,[191] turns out to be very annoyed when someone asks her how many cases they have documented and demands to be believed just because she says something. "Am I the one who needs to provide the evidence for the terrorists' deeds? What kind of travesty is it that they are imposing the burden of proof on me?" she asks, and one wonders who, if not she who has taken on this work, should provide the evidence? In *The New York Times* article on Gal's family, Moshe Fintzy, the deputy police chief, and spokesman for the Israeli police, says "'We have zero autopsies, zero,' making an O with his right hand".

One cannot come to any other conclusion than that the Israeli government and military leadership have deliberately and systematically tried to prevent the truth from coming out, which can be said to be the normal procedure of a belligerent party in a war. The US and the EU have been duped by the Israeli authorities but have also been complicit by parroting without questioning or demanding evidence. The media must take great responsibility for not investigating and questioning, for acting as a megaphone for propaganda and disinformation, and for assembling sensationalist "productions" that can be torn apart by critical analysis.

The responsibility of the media is illustrated by an anecdote in the Israeli journalist Gideon Levy's book *Gaza, My Beloved*:

> *Once a correspondent from French television Channel 1 joined us: at the door of a house in Rafah, at the place where a disabled Palestinian mother lost her only daughter when she was hit by an Israeli missile, I said to the French correspondent: 'Right now I am ashamed to be an Israeli. That horrible missile was also fired in my name.' The next day the correspondent called me: 'We cannot broadcast what you said. Your words are too extreme and our viewers might get angry.' I was deeply hurt. This is exactly what I have been trying to do all these years: to provoke anger.*

One of the most shocking experiences during the writing of this book was watching and listening to an IDF presentation two days after soldiers killed three of the hostages waving a white flag on December 15, 2023, in Gaza. Israel's Commander-in-Chief, General Halevi, met with officers and soldiers of the 99th Division and urged them not to stop thinking, the war is fought not only with the hands and feet but also with the head. He seemed to be most upset that his soldiers were so trigger happy – better to capture enemies so we can get information from them, says the General. Dutifully, he also says that we don't shoot at anyone who has laid down their weapons. But what was really shocking was the statement by female Major Keren Hajioff made in English – intended for audiences abroad – about "The IDF's Robust System for Operational Conduct".[192] In it, the Major makes several accusations against the "savage enemy" Hamas. "…it is difficult to understand to what extremes they go to kill Israelis". These are familiar charges: the use of human shields, ambushes, hiding weapons in incubators, etc. But she took the prize when she lamented that Hamas had destroyed the Erez crossing:

> *a crossing built for the benefit of the people of Gaza, which Gazans used to enter Israel to work, get medical treatment or visit family. The Erez humanitarian crossing was a source of progress and hope until the terrible massacre on October 7, when Hamas destroyed it and killed and kidnapped some of the very people who were stationed there to provide humanitarian aid and assist Gazans.*

Does she understand what she is saying? The Gaza prison door – a source of progress and hope? Does she believe this?

Then she concludes with these words: "Although it is urgent [to crush Hamas and free the hostages], we will pursue it with caution and commitment to the sanctity of life, both Israeli and Palestinian."

I searched in vain for an adjective but remembered that I had promised myself to use as few adjectives as possible and gave up.

Part of the Israeli propaganda campaign is also to accuse "the others" of being "liars and conspiracy theorists". Take, for example, *NBC News's* headline on November 18: "Misinformation has led to questions about Israel's credibility – Israel has published several inaccurate or disputed pieces of information, leading to weakened credibility and online ridicule."[193] The most famous example is the calendar on a wall in al-Shifa hospital that generated a flood of jokes on the internet. More seriously, Ofir Gendelman, Netanyahu's spokesperson for Arab media, posted a video on X (Twitter) that he said showed Gazans faking their injuries with makeup. "The Palestinians are deceiving the international media and public opinion. Don't believe it. See for yourself how they fake injuries and evacuate 39 civilians, all in front of the cameras". Crowds of people rushed to show that the video clip was taken from a Lebanese movie. This is not the first time he has done this. In May 2021, the *BBC* revealed that "a video showing Hamas firing rockets from densely populated areas" was taken during an operation by the Syrian government in Daraa in 2018.[194] *Business Insider* exposed false claims made by *The Jerusalem Post* that a Palestinian grandfather allegedly posed with a doll to accuse Israel of killing his grandchildren, but it was in fact his dead grandchild.[195] *The Post* removed the article about the "doll" but did not publish a retraction. Possibly reasoning along the lines of the *Hasbara* propaganda manual,[196] that "uncritical listeners believe what they hear first and hear often". On December 11, 2023, Swedish public broadcaster *SVT* revealed that "Anders filmed a Swedish bunker – and used this as propaganda in the war. A clip on social media with millions of views claims this to be Hamas's tunnels under Gaza. But the clip actually comes from adventurer Anders Högström from Karlskrona who filmed a Swedish bunker a year ago."[197]

A peculiar argument, rather worn out today but used for a long time, was that the Arab states wanted to keep the Palestinians as refugees and use them to pressurize Israel, as a pawn in the game against the enemy. Instead of being accorded rights in the countries they settled, they have been forced to suffer an unbearable existence. In reality, Palestinians living in Jordan were given citizenship and in Syria and other countries they were given residence and work permits and other rights.

The argument has resurfaced again. The Jewish Policy Centre argues that Egypt is not letting Gazans into the Sinai,

> *which is quite empty… hundreds of thousands of Palestinian civilians are at the town of Rafah near the Philadelphia corridor – the area between northern Sinai and the southern Gaza Strip… According to the principle that the nearest safe place is the best place, could the refugees enter Egypt temporarily? NO, says President Al-Sisi. NO, says UNRWA. NO, says the US government. Why not? Because they are Palestinians and must stay in Palestine – which sounds more like a prison sentence than an attempt to help.*

This seems reasonable. Why not? The problem is that it does not take into account what these refugees want. Palestinians in Arab and other countries want to remain Palestinians. *And it is exactly this that Israel cannot tolerate.* Golda Meir, Minister from 1949 and Prime Minister from 1969 to 1974, said that "there has never been a Palestinian people". Invisibility, dehumanization, and demonization are important steps in the process of denying the Palestinians all their rights, first and foremost the right to self-determination. The settler colonialism projects have always acted in the same way: the aboriginal population must be eliminated, either physically or as a group, that is, it must give up its identity and renounce its right to remain an independent entity. Each case is unique with specific circumstances, but in this respect the Jewish colonization of Palestine is no different from the European settler colonization of South and North America, Australia, New Zealand, South Africa, and Algeria. Complete extermination of a population probably only happened in Tasmania. What Israel cannot tolerate is that Palestinians want to remain Palestinians. This is exactly what is stated in the fundamental law "Israel as the Nation-State of the Jewish People" adopted by the Knesset in 2018. Only Jews have the right to self-determination.

A few words on the Terminology used in the Book

Is what is happening in Gaza a war? Ilan Pappé argues that the word is incorrect and prefers to speak of an "incremental genocide".[198]

Are there two armies fighting? On the Israeli side, troops, soldiers, and officers are appropriate terms, but how should we refer to those fighting on the other side? The book does not use the word terrorists because it implies moral condemnation and disqualification. Palestinian journalists call them "freedom fighters" or "Palestinian fighters".

Are two states fighting? Can we call everyone who fights soldiers and troops?

Is Gaza, which has almost twice the population of Estonia, on one tenth of its surface, a state?

In the text, I have tried not to use the word hostage or kidnapped to describe those imprisoned in Gaza. The Israeli army systematically imprisons Palestinians, including children, who are tried in military courts where almost 100% of the defendants are convicted, or imprisoned in so-called "administrative detention" without charge or trial, sometimes for years. We call them prisoners, not hostages. The thousands who Israel has detained in the West Bank and Gaza since October 7, with the apparent aim of using them in prisoner exchange negotiations with Hamas, the press calls prisoners, not hostages. The press may call them political prisoners, but prisoners, nonetheless. One does not use the word hostage or kidnapping when the act is committed by the State of Israel – with one exception, Israeli journalist Gideon Levy from the *Haaretz* newspaper wonders: "Will Hamas release its hostages faster if Israel mistreats the Palestinians it holds hostage?"[199]

The Geneva Conventions were created, in part, to protect civilians and other non-combatants, including prisoners of war and soldiers who have laid down their arms. They should no longer be legitimate targets of military hostilities, as enemy military personnel are. Should we then say that all those killed on October 7 were murdered, or does this only apply to Israeli civilians? "Israeli soldiers were murdered by Hamas on October 7," says the IDF. Have Hamas men also been murdered? To my knowledge, no one has asked how many there were. They are apparently regarded as suicide bombers. Their deaths need not concern us.

On Wednesday, November 29, 2023, in Jenin, in the northern West Bank, during a ceasefire in Gaza, Adam Samer al-Ghoul, 8 years old, was killed by an Israeli soldier who shot him in the head from behind at a distance of about 10 metres.

Even pro-Palestinian journalists hesitate to use the word murder. When a state kills, it is usually called extrajudicial execution[200] – not murder. When Palestinians attack soldiers at roadblocks, or anywhere else, the victims are referred to as murdered, but when Israel kills civilians, they use the word "killed".

Apparently, the terminology depends on who is responsible for the deed. If it is Palestinians, certain words are generally used, if it is Israel, other words are used.

My research on my own family led me to Theresienstadt, Sobibor, and other concentration camps. Some of my grandfather's second and third cousins, their children and grandchildren, took their lives in desperation in late 1941. Others were murdered in death camps, still others probably succumbed to exhaustion or age in Theresienstadt, a camp used by the Nazis for propaganda purposes to try to counteract the rumours going around Europe about the Nazi treatment of the Jews. But people who died in the Holocaust, even if they died from exhaustion or illness, are always said to have been murdered, and it's not difficult to agree – it's hard to imagine a "natural" death in such a context.

If a person was killed in crossfire during the fighting on October 7, should we call it murder? If so, which side is responsible? Can we say accidental death? Collateral damage?

The wall and fence that surrounds the entire Gaza Strip is in this book called "the barrier" for lack of a better word. The civilians who ran through the breached barrier are referred to in the book as Gazan civilians and not terrorists, even those who killed and wounded civilians, and took civilians hostages into Gaza. The book does not use the word murder, but kill. Not terrorist but Hamas man or militiaman. In quotes, the original text has of course been respected.

Closing words: A Personal Reflection

It is a very strange paradox that we in the West are alarmed by the contemporary tendency in the Middle East to lean towards Islam, but consider it perfectly acceptable for Israel to claim to base the right to its land on a religious scripture and act as if it had a divine mandate – as if to say, "who is the UN to question God?"

Israeli propagandists, as an argument for this or that, tend to claim that there has never been a Palestinian state. In fact, this is completely irrelevant. One hundred and fifty years ago, there was no Israeli state, and most Jews did not know of any country other than the Russian Empire or Hesse, the Netherlands, England, a growing group in the United States, and indeed, Persia, Iraq, Morocco, Egypt, Yemen, and Ethiopia. Palestinians have been made a nation by the last 150 years of history. Nothing strange about that. Is it so different for the Jews?

According to Gideon Levy, the Jews still see themselves as God's chosen people and the land as God-given (Isaac Asimov wrote that this should be distrusted – it was the Jews themselves who wrote it). In some strange way, Christians agree, but we fear the presence of Islam in the politics of the Middle East.

Historian Ervand Abrahamian argues that the 1953 coup in Iran that deposed the democratically elected nationalist Mohammed Mossadegh, crushed the left and helped to destroy nationalism, socialism, and liberalism as valid ideologies for change. Only religion remained. "The roots of Khomeini's 1979 Islamist revolution lie in the events of 1953," he writes. Something similar happened in Palestine. The West demanded democracy from the Palestinians. Arafat had no problem with this. The PLO won elections in the occupied territories in the 1970s. Hamas, probably reluctant to accept Western democracy, finally agreed and participated in the 2005 local elections and the 2006 parliamentary elections. And won. And what happened?

Well, neither Israel, the EU, nor the US could tolerate this. They helped Palestinian President Mahmoud Abbas try to steal power from Hamas, who responded by taking power in Gaza.

Arafat was a left-leaning nationalist but after his death the Palestinian Authority with Abbas became the darling of the US – liberal and "democratic". Is it any wonder that Hamas says, "God is greatest" and "God will help us?"

Where do we stand now? The situation seems hopeless. Perhaps South Africa's indictment of Israel for genocide in the ICJ may offer openings. Maybe Netanyahu will be deposed by the army in a coup, a popular uprising, or new elections. However, a new government will probably not mean major, immediate changes. Militarily, Israel seems to have failed to achieve its objective to destroy Hamas (which reportedly still offers stiff resistance – Israeli soldiers are still killed and wounded in Gaza – and is supported by a tormented people). The only thing Israel has managed to do is to kill and maim people, destroy houses and infrastructure, obliterate health services, schools and universities, cause a famine, and force the population of Gaza into a corner of the Gaza Strip on the border with Egypt. And to alienate itself from the whole world. One may ask who it is behaving as "merchants of hate" driven by "vengeful pathologies".

What is clear is that neither Palestine, the Middle East, nor the world will be the same after October 7. Hamas punched Israel right in the face of its strongest myth, in its solar plexus – the invincibility of its army, the IDF. Israel's masculinity has been humiliated, wrote Yael Hallak in *Haaretz*,[201] and the answer is violence. Burg's words resound: "Israel has force, lots of force and nothing but force".

The former head of the *Shin Bet*, Ami Ayalon, has proposed releasing all Palestinian prisoners including, Marwan Barghouti, who he considers the only one who can be elected and is capable of leading the Palestinians.[202]

> *The misconception was that the Palestinians aren't a people, and if we allow them to have economic prosperity, they'll give up the dream of independence. In the end, the Palestinians define themselves as a people. They're willing to kill and be killed for their independence, and the terrorists who are killed turn into martyrs in their eyes.*

It is hard to imagine that Israel can survive in its present form, legally, geographically, socially, and politically, after October 7 and the events in Gaza. The changes that will come cannot be predicted, but the blockade of Gaza and an increasingly open racist and aggressive settler movement in the West Bank will not be able to last. The transformation will affect not only Israel and Palestine and the whole region, but also the US and the EU and probably the world.

Hannah Arendt's words on the first page of this book sound unfortunately prophetic.

> *Some of the Zionists leaders pretend to believe that the Jews can maintain themselves in Palestine against the whole world and that they them-*

Now we are here. Israel has the ability to solve this, it just needs to leave the master race mentality behind, its exceptionalism and messianism. Israel must just realize that there is nothing special about belonging to this or that religion, that you cannot live your life with dignity if you do not respect the dignity of your fellow human beings. Stop fooling themselves with arguments like "they started it" or "we are just defending ourselves". Israel is not fighting for its self-determination in Gaza – as many journalists and probably some Israelis believe – but to maintain its own image of being invincible, "a wall against barbarism".

I tried myself to understand what it means to be Jewish. I wanted to understand how my grandfather felt when he was baptized in 1890 in Berlin to get the job he wanted, what he thought when he married an extremely conservative Catholic girl half his age in Buenos Aires in 1915. I was raised in an extremely conservative Catholic family. My approach to Judaism was not motivated by religion, but by anger because my father had kept my grandfather's Jewishness a secret for so many years and that so many in my family find the Jewish connection problematic. I promised myself to get to the bottom of it, sought out Jewish relatives and talked at length with them. They gave me advice on what to read. After a while, they asked me if it was time for a Bar Mitzvah. "I am not a believer," was my short answer. I don't believe in any god, neither the God of the Jews, nor the Christians, not the Muslims, who, although most people don't know it, are one and the same. I do not believe in the gods of any heaven, Nirvana, or even a sacred earth.

My grandmother – who married a man born and probably even raised as a Jew – shared the prejudice against Jews that prevailed in Catholic Spain and its colonies. As a child, I found this difficult to understand and thought that we Christians had every reason to thank the Jews for allowing Jesus to die on the cross. Without which event, God's plan could not have been realized, and humanity saved and we would have had to continue living without knowing the true God. Of course, I never dared to ask my grandmother about this.

My grandfather was lucky enough to die in 1938, so he did not have to see his once beloved Germany go to war with the rest of Europe and his cousins and their children taken to Theresienstadt and on to Auschwitz, Sobibor, and other death camps. Poor grandfather! During World War I, he indignantly left the fine Club Uruguay after some gentlemen there repeated the Allies' atrocity propaganda that German soldiers in Belgium were killing and eating the children. Twenty years later, he resigned his membership of the Deutscher Klub in Montevideo when the club replaced Bismarck's portrait with Hitler's and members stopped making jokes about "der *schöne* Adolf" (the Germans used to joke about the "ridiculous" little Austrian corporal until he came to power!). Some of my grandfather's relatives in Kassel managed to escape in time. After the lawyer Max Plaut was murdered by the Nazis in the Burgersäle in Kassel in March 1933, his brother Ernst Philip fled to Palestine, but his mother Henriette Katzenstein stayed in Kassel where she lived at Kaiserstrasse 13, next door to her friend and relative Franziska Katzenstein (née Plaut), mother of the aviator Kurt Katzenstein, who fled first to Holland and then to South Africa, where a few years later he changed his surname to Kaye. I wonder if Franziska even tried to stay in South Africa when she visited her son there in 1938. Why didn't Henriette accompany Ernst Philip to Palestine? Henriette's sister Fanny was married to Max Feldstein, also a second cousin of my grandfather (most Jews in Kassel were related to each other). Max and Fanny owned a textile factory that produced uniforms. Their factory was confiscated, and the situation became so desperate that they killed themselves together in the village of Britenau on November 15, 1941. They were 77 and 79 years old, respectively.

When I walked the cobbled streets of Theresienstadt in the mid-1990s, I did not know that Franziska and Henriette had walked on the same stones with tired feet when they were deported there on September 7, 1942. Both died there. Could some of the soldiers guarding the ghetto have had uniforms that came from Max Feldstein's factory? Another sister of Henriette, Ida, was deported to Theresienstadt. Max and Fanny's daughter Ella lived in Berlin and escaped to Yugoslavia, but when the Nazis invaded, she was sent to a death camp.

Would my experience of the Theresienstadt ghetto have been different if I had known that so many relatives had died there or been deported further? Some of the prisoners in Theresienstadt could have been called Wallach, Ganz, Rothschild, Katzenstein, Weiss, or something else, related to me or not. Aren't we all, in the end, cousins to each other? Among the prisoners in Theresienstadt, there were heroes who organized children's activities and took care of the sick and in a thousand ways preserved what dignity could be preserved.

Others were depressed people who could only mourn their parents, siblings, or friends whom they had seen tortured or murdered and were resigned to their own death. Perhaps someone had broken down under torture and agreed to spy on their fellow prisoners. Another could not resist the temptation to steal food from the sick in order to survive or make money by selling the bread he had found. Victims don't have to be heroes, although we like to think so. We honour them because they suffered – but not us.

We humans are strange. Suffering can become a merit. During the harsh years in Uruguay, when people were dying from police bullets in demonstrations or being tortured to death in military barracks, political groups competed to see who had the most prisoners, most killed, most wanted people. As if the enemy's brutality was proof that they were right. Nothing new under the sun. Martyrdom is so central to Christianity that salvation itself comes through death and the religion has as its symbol an instrument of torture and execution. Martyrdom was the ultimate proof of piety. It is as if we believed that being a victim is the victim's "own merit". That may be so, but often it is chance that decides. If a police bullet shatters someone's liver or brain during a demonstration, the dead person is no better than the one who was half a metre to the right or left, and no better than she herself was half a second before the bullet took her life. When we honour the dead, we cannot help but make them saints, especially if it can give us some of the light that radiates from every saint. Among us refugees, it was common to cherish our years in prison as the most precious medal that says, "former political prisoner", a glorious merit that not everyone can show. We want to see the victims as free from every possible stain and the perpetrator as evil itself.

And what did I learn about Judaism? That it is a faith like any other, and no matter how hard I tried, I could never figure out anything special about being Jewish. Jews are people like everyone else, they believe in their God and their scriptures, but they are no different from anyone else and have no more or less rights than any other people on this troubled earth.

What I want is for my friends and relatives in Tel Aviv and elsewhere in Israel, and many others, to take the bus to Ramallah, Bethlehem, and Hebron, Nablus, Tulkarm, and Jericho, or why not to Rafah, and Gaza City, and Khan Younis, and spend a week with a family, doing internships in hospitals, schools, and workshops, and going to the olive harvest and the fields. And realize that there is no difference between Palestinians and Jews either.

Acknowledgments

As far as possible, I have used Israeli and Western sources (newspapers, magazines, TV, etc.), many of these mainstream media but also *Aljazeera*, which has proved to be a serious and reliable news site, the Israeli organization *B'tselem*, *+972magazine* and others.

The Electronic Intifada, a US site run by Ali Abunimah, has been indispensable, not least because David Sheen and Dena Shunra have translated countless interviews and articles from Hebrew newspapers. *The Electronic Intifada* has shown great integrity and accuracy in its reporting and analysis.

Other sources I have used extensively are *Middle East Eye*, a news site founded by David Hearst, a former Guardian journalist, and *Mondoweiss*, run by Philip Weiss and David Horowitz, which covers the region from a "progressive Jewish perspective".

Thanks to Adnan Abu-Chackra for reading the manuscript and making relevant comments, to Tim Houghton who reviewed the English version, and to Christer Bergström, publisher at Vaktel Books.

All errors and mistakes are only mine.

And thanks to Mary, who has been so patient with me when I disappear behind the books and papers or sink into the computer screen, and who has read and commented and encouraged.

Appendix I
Hamas's own statement on October 7

So far, I have mainly concentrated on the Israeli version and narratives of October 7. For the sake of balance, I reproduce here an extract from the document, *Our Narrative… Operation Al-Aqsa Flood*, published by Hamas in mid-January 2024. The Israeli version has an almost complete monopoly in the Western media. It is therefore important for a historical account – which this book actually is – to give the other side's view of what happened. Anything else would be contrary to good historiographical tradition and morality. The aim is not to say that Hamas is right. Insofar as what is claimed by Hamas in the following text needs to be commented on, this has been done explicitly earlier in this book. There is no underlying political purpose in publishing this excerpt – this book is pure history, with no political purpose. The only purpose is to give the reader another perspective on what happened. We leave the conclusions to the reader.

The excerpt from the report follows below; the full report can be read at https://www.palestinechronicle.com/hamas-document-reveals-why-we-we-carried-out-al-aqsa-flood-operation-summary-pdf/.

First: Why Operation Al-Aqsa Flood?

1. The battle of the Palestinian people against occupation and colonialism did not start on Oct. 7, but started 105 years ago, including 30 years of British colonialism and 75 years of Zionist occupation. In 1918, the Palestinian people owned 98.5% of the Palestine land and represented 92% of the population on the land of Palestine. While the Jews, who were brought to Palestine in mass immigration campaigns in coordination between the British colonial authorities and the Zionist Movement, managed to seize control of not more than 6% of the lands in Palestine and to be 31% of the population prior to 1948 when the Zionist Entity was announced on the historic land of Palestine. At that time, the Palestinian people were denied from the right to self-determination and the Zionist gangs engaged in an ethnic cleansing campaign against the Palestinian people aimed at expelling them from their lands and areas. As a result, the Zionist gangs seized control by force of 77% of the land of Palestine where they

expelled 57% of the people of Palestine* and destroyed over 500 Palestinian villages and towns and committed dozens of massacres against the Palestinians which all culminated in the establishment of the Zionist Entity in 1948. Moreover, in continuation of the aggression, the Israeli forces in 1967 occupied the rest of Palestine including the West Bank, the Gaza Strip and Jerusalem in addition to Arab territories around Palestine.

2. Over these long decades, the Palestinian people suffered all forms of oppression, injustice, expropriation of their fundamental rights and the apartheid policies. The Gaza Strip, for example, suffered as of 2007 from a suffocating blockade over 17 years which turned it to be the largest open-air prison in the world. The Palestinian people in Gaza also suffered from five destructive wars/aggressions all of which "Israel" was the offending party. The people in Gaza in 2018 also initiated the Great March of Return demonstrations to peacefully protest the Israeli blockade, their miserable humanitarian conditions and to demand their right-to-return.

However, the Israeli occupation forces responded to these protests with brutal force by which 360 Palestinians were killed and 19,000 others were injured including over 5,000 children in a matter of few months.

3. According to official figures, in the period between (January 2000 and September 2023), the Israeli occupation killed 11,299 Palestinians and injured 156,768 others, the great majority of them were civilians. Unfortunately, the US administration and its allies did not pay attention to the suffering of the Palestinian people over the past years but provided cover to the Israeli aggression. They only lamented the Israeli soldiers who were killed on Oct. 7 even without seeking the truth of what happened, and wrongfully walked behind the Israeli narrative in condemning an alleged targeting of Israeli civilians. The US administration provided the financial and military support to the Israeli occupation massacres against the Palestinian civilians and the brutal aggression on the Gaza Strip, and still the US officials continue to ignore what the Israeli occupation forces commit in Gaza of mass killing.

---

* In the Glossary and the text, it is stated that the Zionist militias "displaced 80% of the Palestinians". This 80% refers to the territories that became the state of Israel, the international recognized borders from the Armistice 1949 (the Green Line). Hamas 57 % refers to the whole Palestinian population in the historic Palestine (the British Mandate Palestine).

4. The Israeli violations and brutality were documented by many UN organizations and international human rights groups including Amnesty International and Human Rights Watch, and even documented by Israeli human rights groups. However, these reports and testimonies were ignored and the Israeli occupation is yet to be held accountable. For example, on Oct. 29, 2021, Israel's Ambassador to the UN Gilad Erdan insulted the UN system by tearing up a report for the UN Human Rights Council during an address at the General Assembly and threw it in a dustbin before leaving the podium. Yet, he was appointed in the following year – 2022 – to the post of vice-president of the UN General Assembly.

5. The US administration and its western allies have always been treating Israel as a state above the law; they provide it with the needed cover to maintain prolonging the occupation and cracking down the Palestinian people, and also allowing "Israel" to exploit such situation to expropriate further Palestinian lands and to Judaize their sanctities and holy sites. Despite the fact that the UN had issued more than 900 resolutions over the past 75 years in favour of the Palestinian people, "Israel" rejected to abide by any of these resolutions, and the US VETO was always present at the UN Security Council to prevent any condemnation to "Israel's" policies and violations. That's why we see the US and other western countries complicit and partners to the Israeli occupation in its crimes and in the continued suffering of the Palestinian people.

6. As for "the peaceful settlement process". Despite the fact that the Oslo Accords signed in 1993 with the Palestine Liberation Organization (PLO) stipulated the establishment of a Palestinian independent state in the West Bank and the Gaza Strip; "Israel" systematically destroyed every possibility to establish the Palestinian state through a wide campaign of settlements' construction and Judaization of the Palestinian lands in the occupied West Bank and Jerusalem. The backers of the peace process after 30 years realized that they have reached an impasse and that such process had catastrophic results on the Palestinian people. The Israeli officials confirmed on several occasions their absolute rejection to the establishment of a Palestinian state. Just one month before Operation Al-Aqsa Flood, Israeli Prime Minister Benjamin Netanyahu presented a map of a so-called "New Middle East," depicting "Israel" stretching from the Jordan River to the Mediterranean Sea including the West Bank and Gaza. The entire world at that – UN General Assembly's – podium were silent towards his speech full of arrogance and ignorance towards the rights of the Palestinian people.

7. After 75 years of relentless occupation and suffering, and after failing all initiatives for liberation and return to our people, and also after the disastrous results of the so-called peace process, what did the world expect from the Palestinian people to do in response to the following:

♦ The Israeli Judaization plans to the blessed Al-Aqsa Mosque, its temporal and spatial division attempts, as well as the intensification of the Israeli settlers' incursions into the holy mosque.

♦ The practices of the extremist and right-wing Israeli government which is practically taking steps towards annexing the entire West Bank and Jerusalem into the so-called "Israel's sovereignty" amid plans on the Israeli official table to expel Palestinians from their homes and areas.

♦ The thousands of Palestinian detainees in Israeli jails who are experiencing deprivation of their basic rights as well as assaults and humiliations under direct supervision of the Israeli fascist minister Itamar Ben-Gvir.

♦ The unjust air, sea, and land blockade imposed on the Gaza Strip over 17 years.

♦ The expansion of the Israeli settlements across the West Bank in an unprecedented level, as well as the daily violence perpetrated by settlers against Palestinians and their properties.

♦ The seven million Palestinians living in extreme conditions in refugee camps and other areas who wish to return to their lands, and who were expelled 75 years ago.

♦ The failure of the international community and the complicity of super-powers to prevent the establishment of a Palestinian state.

What was expected from the Palestinian people after all of that? To keep waiting and to keep counting on the helpless UN! Or to take the initiative in defending the Palestinian people, lands, rights and sanctities; knowing that the defence act is a right enshrined in international laws, norms and conventions.

Proceeding from the above, Operation Al-Aqsa Flood on Oct. 7 was a necessary step and a normal response to confront all Israeli conspiracies against the Palestinian people and their cause. It was a defensive act in the frame of getting rid of the Israeli occupation, reclaiming the Palestinian rights and on the way for liberation and independence like all peoples around the world did.

Second: The events of Operation Al-Aqsa Flood and responses to the Israeli allegations

In light of the Israeli fabricated accusations and allegations over Operation Al-Aqsa Flood on Oct. 7 and its repercussions, we in the Islamic Resistance Movement – Hamas clarify the following:

1. Operation Al-Aqsa Flood on Oct. 7 targeted the Israeli military sites and sought to arrest the enemy's soldiers to pressure on the Israeli authorities to release the thousands of Palestinians held in Israeli jails through a prisoners exchange deal. Therefore, the operation focused on destroying the Israeli army's Gaza Division, the Israeli military sites stationed near the Israeli settlements around Gaza.

2. Avoiding harm to civilians, especially children, women and elderly people is a religious and moral commitment by all the Al-Qassam Brigades' fighters. We reiterate that the Palestinian resistance was fully disciplined and committed to the Islamic values during the operation and that the Palestinian fighters only targeted the occupation soldiers and those who carried weapons against our people. In the meantime, the Palestinian fighters were keen to avoid harming civilians despite the fact that the resistance does not possess precise weapons. In addition, if there was any case of targeting civilians; it happened accidently and in the course of the confrontation with the occupation forces.

Since its establishment in 1987, the Hamas Movement committed itself to avoiding harm to civilians. After Zionist criminal Baruch Goldstein in 1994 committed a massacre against Palestinian worshippers in the Al-Ibrahimi Mosque in occupied Hebron City, the Hamas Movement announced an initiative to avoid civilians the brunt of fighting by all parties, but the Israeli occupation rejected it and even did not give any comment on it. The Hamas Movement also repeated such calls several times, but received by a deaf ear from the Israeli occupation which continued its deliberate targeting and killing of Palestinian civilians.

3. Maybe some faults happened during Operation Al-Aqsa Flood's implementation due to the rapid collapse of the Israeli security and military system, and the chaos caused along the border areas with Gaza.

As attested by many, the Hamas Movement dealt in a positive and kind manner with all civilians who have been held in Gaza and sought from the earliest days of the aggression to release them, and that's what happened during the week-long humanitarian truce where those civilians were released in exchange of releasing Palestinian women and children from Israeli jails.

4. What the Israeli occupation promoted of allegations that the Al-Qassam Brigades on Oct. 7 were targeting Israeli civilians are nothing but complete lies and fabrications. The source of these allegations is the Israeli official narrative and no independent source proved any of them. It is a well-known fact that the Israeli official narrative had always sought to demonize the Palestinian resistance, while also legalizing its brutal aggression on Gaza.

Here are some details that go against the Israeli allegations:

- Video clips taken on that day – Oct. 7 – along with the testimonies by Israelis themselves that were released later showed that the Al-Qassam Brigades' fighters didn't target civilians, and many Israelis were killed by the Israeli army and police due to their confusion.

- It has also been firmly refuted the lie of the "40 beheaded babies" by the Palestinian fighters, and even Israeli sources denied this lie. Many of the western media agencies unfortunately adopted this allegation and promoted it.

- The suggestion that the Palestinian fighters committed rape against Israeli women was fully denied including by the Hamas Movement. A report by the Mondoweiss news website on Dec. 1, 2023, among others, said there is lack of any evidence of "mass rape" allegedly perpetrated by Hamas members on Oct. 7 and that Israel used such allegation "to fuel the genocide in Gaza."

- According to two reports by the Israeli Yedioth Ahronoth newspaper on Oct. 10 and the Haaretz newspaper on Nov. 18, many Israeli civilians were killed by an Israeli military helicopter especially those who were in the Nova music festival near Gaza where 364 Israeli civilians were killed. The two reports said the Hamas fighters reached the area of the festival without any prior knowledge of the festival, where the Israeli helicopter opened fire on both the Hamas fighters and the participants in the festival. The Yedioth Ahronoth also said the Israeli army, to prevent further infiltrations from Gaza and to prevent any Israelis being arrested by the Palestinian fighters, struck over 300 targets in areas surrounding the Gaza Strip.

- Other Israeli testimonies confirmed that the Israeli army raids and soldiers' operations killed many Israeli captives and their captors. The Israeli occupation army bombed the houses in the Israeli settlements where Palestinian fighters and Israelis were inside in a clear application of the Israeli army notorious "Hannibal Directive" which clearly says that "better a dead civilian hostage or soldier than taken alive" to avoid engaging in a prisoner swap with the Palestinian resistance.

- Furthermore, the occupation authorities revised the number of their killed soldiers and civilians from 1,400 to 1,200, after finding that 200-burnt corpses had belonged to the Palestinian fighters who were killed and mixed with Israeli corpses. This means that the one who killed the fighters is the one who killed the Israelis, knowing that only the Israeli army possesses military planes that killed, burned and destroyed Israeli areas on Oct. 7.

- The Israeli heavy aerial raids across Gaza that led to the death of nearly 60 Israeli captives also prove that the Israeli occupation does not care about the life of their captives in Gaza.

5. Det är också ett faktum att ett antal israeliska bosättare i bosättningar runt 5. It is also a matter of fact that several Israeli settlers in settlements around Gaza were armed, and clashed with Palestinian fighters on Oct. 7. Those settlers were registered as civilians while the fact is they were armed men fighting alongside the Israeli army.

6. When speaking about Israeli civilians, it must be known that conscription applies to all Israelis above the age of 18 – males who served 32 months of military service and females who served 24 months – where all can carry and use arms. This is based on the Israeli security theory of an "armed people" which turned the Israeli entity into "an army with a country attached."

7. The brutal killing of civilians is a systematic approach of the Israeli entity, and one of the means to humiliate the Palestinian people. The mass killing of Palestinians in Gaza is clear evidence of such an approach.

8. The Al Jazeera news channel said in a documentary that in one month of the Israeli aggression on Gaza, the daily average killing of Palestinian children in Gaza was 136, while the average of children killing in Ukraine – in the course of the Russian-Ukrainian war – was one child every day.

9. Those who defend the Israeli aggression do not look at the events in an objective manner but rather go to justify the Israeli mass killing of Palestinians by saying there would be casualties among civilians when attacking the Hamas fighters. However, they would not use such assumption when it comes to the Al-Aqsa Flood event on Oct. 7.

10. We are confident that any fair and independent inquiries will prove the truth of our narrative and will prove the scale of lies and misleading information in the Israeli side. This also includes the Israeli allegations regarding the hospitals in Gaza that the Palestinian resistance used them as command centres; an allegation that was not proven and was refuted by reports of many western press agencies.

Third: Towards a transparent international investigation

1. Palestine is a member-state of the International Criminal Court (ICC) and it acceded to its Rome Statute in 2015. When Palestine asked for investigation into Israeli war crimes committed on its territories, it was faced by Israeli intransigence and rejection, and threats to punish the Palestinians for the request to ICC. It is also unfortunate to mention that there were great powers, which claim to be holding values of justice, completely sided with the occupation narrative and stood against the Palestinian moves in the international justice system. These powers want to keep "Israel" as a state above the law and to ensure it escapes liability and accountability.

2. We urge these countries, especially the US administration, Germany, Canada and the UK, if they mean for justice to prevail as they claim, they ought to announce their support to the course of the investigation in all crimes committed in occupied Palestine and to give full support for the international courts to effectively do their job.

3. Despite having doubts from these countries to stand by justice, we still urge the ICC Prosecutor and his team to immediately and urgently come to occupied Palestine to look into the crimes and violations committed there, rather than merely observing the situation remotely or being subject to the Israeli restrictions.

4. In Dec. 2022, when the UN General Assembly passed a resolution seeking opinion of the International Court of Justice (ICJ) on the legal consequences of "Israel's" illegal occupation of Palestinian territories, those (few) countries who back "Israel" announced their rejection to the move that was approved by nearly 100 countries. And when our people – and their legal and rights groups – sought to pursue prosecutions against the Israeli war criminals in front of the European countries courts – through the system of universal jurisdiction – the European regimes obstructed the moves in favour of the Israeli war criminals to remain running free.

5. The events of Oct. 7 must be put in its broader context, and that all cases of struggle against colonialism and occupation in our contemporary time be evoked. These experiences of struggle show that in the same level of oppression committed by the occupier; there would be an equivalent response by the people under occupation.

6. The Palestinian people and peoples across the world realize the scale of lies and deception these governments that back the Israeli narrative practice in their attempts to justify their blind bias and to cover the Israeli crimes. These countries know the root causes of the conflict which are the occupation and the denial of the right of the Palestinian people to live in dignity on their lands. These countries show no interest towards the continuation of the unjust blockade on millions of Palestinians in Gaza, and also show no interest towards the thousands of Palestinian detainees in Israeli jails held under conditions where their basic rights are mostly denied.

7. We hail the free people of the world from all religions, ethnicities and backgrounds who rally in all capitals and cities worldwide to voice their rejection to the Israeli crimes and massacres, and to show their support for the rights of the Palestinian people and their just cause.

Fourth: A reminder to the world, who is Hamas?

1. The Islamic Resistance Movement "Hamas" is a Palestinian Islamic national liberation and resistance movement. Its goal is to liberate Palestine and confront the Zionist project. Its frame of reference is Islam, which determines its principles, objectives and means. Hamas rejects the persecution of any human

being or the undermining of his or her rights on nationalist, religious or sectarian grounds.

2. Hamas affirms that its conflict is with the Zionist project not with the Jews because of their religion. Hamas does not wage a struggle against the Jews because they are Jewish but wages a struggle against the Zionists who occupy Palestine. Yet, it is the Zionists who constantly identify Judaism and the Jews with their own colonial project and illegal entity.

3. The Palestinian people have always stood against oppression, injustice, and the committing of massacres against civilians regardless of who commit them. And based on our religious and moral values, we clearly stated our rejection to what the Jews were exposed to by the Nazi Germany. Here, we remind that the Jewish problem in essence was a European problem, while the Arab and Islamic environment was – across history – a safe haven to the Jewish people and to other peoples of other beliefs and ethnicities. The Arab and Islamic environment was an example to co-existence, cultural interaction and religious freedoms. The current conflict is caused by the Zionist aggressive behaviour and its alliance with the western colonial powers; therefore, we reject the exploitation of the Jewish suffering in Europe to justify the oppression against our people in Palestine.

4. The Hamas Movement according to international laws and norms is a national liberation movement that has clear goals and mission. It gets its legitimacy to resist the occupation from the Palestinian right to self-defence, liberation and self-determination. Hamas has always been keen to restrict its fight and resistance with the Israeli occupation on the occupied Palestinian territory, yet, the Israeli occupation did not abide by that and committed massacres and killings against the Palestinians outside Palestine.

5. We stress that resisting the occupation with all means including the armed resistance is a legitimized right by all norms, divine religions, the international laws including the Geneva Conventions and its first additional protocol and the related UN resolutions e.g. The UN General Assembly Resolution 3236, adopted by the 29th session of the General Assembly on Nov. 22, 1974, which affirmed the inalienable rights of the Palestinian people in Palestine, including the right to self-determination and the right to return to "their homes and property from where they were expelled, displaced and uprooted."

6. Our steadfast Palestinian people and their resistance are waging a heroic battle to defend their land and national rights against the longest and most brutal colonial occupation. The Palestinian people are confronting an unprecedented Israeli aggression that committed heinous massacres against Palestinian civilians, most of them were children and women. In the course of the aggression on Gaza, the Israeli occupation deprived our people in Gaza of food, water, medicines and fuel, and simply deprived them from all means of life. In the meantime, the Israeli warplanes savagely struck all Gaza infrastructures and public buildings including schools, universities, mosques, churches and hospitals in a clear sign of ethnic cleansing aimed at expelling the Palestinian people from Gaza. Yet, the backers of the Israeli occupation did nothing but kept the genocide ongoing against our people.

7. The Israeli occupation's use of the "self-defence" pretext to justify its oppression against the Palestinian people is a process of lie, deception and turning the facts. The Israeli entity has no right to defend its crimes and occupation but the Palestinian people who have such right to oblige the occupier to end the occupation. In 2004, the International Court of Justice (ICJ) gave an advisory opinion in the case concerning the "Legal Consequences of the Construction of a Wall in the Occupied Palestinian Territory" which stated that "Israel" – the brutal occupying force – cannot rely on a right of self-defence to build such wall on the Palestinian territory. Furthermore, Gaza under the international law is still an occupied land, thus, the justifications for waging the aggression on Gaza is baseless and lacks its legal capacity, as well as lacks the essence of the self-defence idea.

Fifth: What is needed?

Occupation is occupation no matter how it describes or names itself, and remains a tool to break the will of the peoples and to keep oppressing them. On the other side, the experiences of the peoples\nations across history on how to break away from occupation and colonialism confirm that the resistance is the strategic approach and the only way to liberation and ending the occupation. Has any nation been liberated from occupation without struggle, resistance or sacrifice?

The humanitarian, ethical and legal imperatives necessitate all countries around the world to back the resistance of the Palestinian people not to collude against it. They are supposed to confront the occupation crimes and aggression, as well as to support the struggle of the Palestinian people to liberate their lands and to practice their right to self-determination like all peoples across the globe. Based on that, we call for the following:

1. The immediate halt of the Israeli aggression on Gaza, the crimes and ethnic cleansing committed against the entire Gaza population, to open the crossings and allow the entry of humanitarian aid into Gaza, including reconstruction tools.

2. To hold the Israeli occupation legally accountable for what it caused of human suffering towards the Palestinian people, and to charge it for the crimes against civilians, infrastructure, hospitals, educational facilities, mosques, and churches.

3. The support of the Palestinian resistance in the face of the Israeli occupation with all possible means as a legitimized right under the international laws and norms.

4. We call upon the free peoples across the world, especially those nations who were colonized and realize the suffering of the Palestinian people, to take serious and effective positions against the double standard policies adopted by powers\countries that back the Israeli occupation. We call on these nations to initiate a global solidarity movement with the Palestinian people and to emphasize the values of justice and equality and the right of the peoples to live in freedom and dignity.

5. The superpowers, especially the US, the UK and France among others, must stop providing the Zionist entity with cover from accountability, and to stop dealing with it as a country above the law. Such unjust behaviour by these countries allowed the Israeli occupation over 75 years to commit the worst crimes ever against the Palestinian people, land and sanctities. We urge the countries across the globe, today and more than before, to uphold their responsibilities towards the international law and the relevant UN resolutions that call for ending the occupation.

6. We categorically reject any international or Israeli projects aimed at deciding the future of Gaza that only serve to prolong the occupation. We stress that the Palestinian people have the capacity to decide their future and to arrange their

internal affairs, and thus no party in the world has the right to impose any form of guardianship on the Palestinian people or decide on their behalf.

7. We urge for standing against the Israeli attempts to cause another wave of expulsion – or a new Nakba – to the Palestinians especially in the lands occupied in 1948 and the West Bank. We stress that there will be no expulsion to Sinai or Jordan or any other place, and if there is any relocation to the Palestinians, it will be towards their homes and areas they were expelled from in 1948, as affirmed by many UN resolutions.

8. We call for keeping the popular pressure around the world until ending the occupation; we call for standing against the normalization attempts with the Israeli entity and for a comprehensive boycott to the Israeli occupation and its backers.

Appendix II

The Likud Charter

The Right of the Jewish People to the Land of Israel (Eretz Israel)

a. The right of the Jewish people to the land of Israel is eternal and indisputable and is linked with the right to security and peace; therefore, Judea and Samaria will not be handed to any foreign administration; between the Sea and the Jordan there will only be Israeli sovereignty.

b. A plan which relinquishes parts of western Eretz Israel, undermines our right to the country, unavoidably leads to the establishment of a "Palestinian State," jeopardizes the security of the Jewish population, endangers the existence of the State of Israel. and frustrates any prospect of peace.

Genuine Peace – Our Central Objective

a. The Likud government will place its aspirations for peace at the top of its priorities and will spare no effort to promote peace. The Likud will act as a genuine partner at peace treaty negotiations with our neighbours, as is customary among the nations. The Likud government will attend the Geneva Conference.

b. The Likud governments peace initiative will be positive. Directly or through a friendly state. Israel will invite her neighbours to hold direct negotiations, in order to sign without pre-conditions on either side and without any solution formula invented by outsiders (invented outside). At the negotiations each party will be free to make any proposals it deems lit.

Settlement

Settlement. both urban and rural. in all parts of the Land of Israel is the focal point of the Zionist effort to redeem the country, to maintain vital security areas and serves as a reservoir of strength and inspiration for the renewal of the pioneering spirit. The Likud government will call on the younger generation in Israel and the dispersions to settle and help every group and individual in the task of inhabiting and cultivating the wasteland, while taking care not to dispossess anyone.

Arab Terror Organizations

The PLO is no national liberation organization but an organization of assassins, which the Arab countries use as a political and military tool, while also serving the interests of Soviet imperialism, to stir up the area. Its aim is to liquidate the State of Israel, set up an Arab country instead and make the Land of Israel part of the Arab world. The Likud government will strive to eliminate these murderous organizations in order to prevent them from carrying out their bloody deeds.

Source: Likud Official Website; Walter Laqueur and Barry Rubin, ed, "The Israel-Arab Reader: A Documentary History of the Middle East Conflict, 6th Edition" (New York, NY: Penguin Books, 2001.

Likud Party Platform (after Oslo)

Preamble

The right of the Jewish people to the Land of Israel is an eternal right, not subject to dispute, and includes the right to security and peace. Zionism is the liberation movement of the Jewish people, and its fulfilment is at the top of the list of priorities of the Government of Israel. Immigration will be increased, and settlement will be strengthened. The decision to freeze settlements will be rescinded. Peace will be a central aim of Israel's policy. The Government of Israel will conduct direct negotiations with Arab states to reach peace agreements. Security is the basis for durable peace in our region. Israel will make security a first condition in any peace agreement.

Operatives

1. The Government of Israel will honour international agreements, and will continue the diplomatic process to achieve a just and lasting peace in the Middle East. It will recognize the facts created on the ground by the various accords, and will act to reduce the dangers to the future and security of Israel resulting from these agreements.

2. The Government of Israel will carry out negotiations with the Palestinian Authority to achieve a permanent peace arrangement, on condition that the Palestinians fully honour all their obligations. Most important among these are

that the Palestinians annul in an unequivocal manner the clauses in the Palestinian Charter which call for the destruction of Israel, and that they prevent terror and incitement against Israel.

3. The Government of Israel will enable the Palestinians to manage their lives freely, within the framework of self-government. However, foreign affairs and defence, and matters which require coordination, will remain the responsibility of the State of Israel. The government will oppose the establishment of an independent Palestinian state.

4. Sources of employment for the Palestinians will be developed in the autonomous areas to reduce the number of Palestinian workers in the Israeli market.

5. Jewish settlement, security areas, water resources, state land and road intersections in Judea, Samaria and the Gaza Strip shall remain under full Israeli control.

6. Israel will keep its vital water resources in Judea and Samaria. There shall be no infringement of Israel's use of its water resources.

7. United and undivided Jerusalem is the capital of the State of Israel. Activities which undermine the status of Jerusalem will be banned, and therefore PLO and Palestinian Authority institutions in the city will be closed.

8. The Jordan River shall be the eastern border of the State of Israel, south of Lake Kinneret. This will be the permanent border between the State of Israel and the Hashemite Kingdom of Jordan. The Kingdom of Jordan may become a partner in the final arrangement between Israel and the Palestinians, in areas agreed upon in the negotiations.

9. Israel will conduct peace negotiations with Syria, while maintaining Israeli sovereignty over the Golan Heights and its water resources.

10. The government will set a goal of having seven million Jews in Israel within the next decade. The government will prepare the country to absorb Jews, both new immigrants and returning citizens, viewing this not only as a national undertaking but as strengthening Israel economically and culturally.

11. Settlement in all parts of the Land of Israel is of national importance and part of Israel's defence strategy. The government will allocate special resources for settlement in border and sparsely-populated areas.

Source: James Madison University, https://educ.jmu.edu/~vannorwc/assets/ ghist%20102-150/pages/arabisraeli/likudpolicy.html

Appendix III
Historical revisionism

Historical revisionism,[*] the distortion of historical facts, is a dangerous weapon in the hands of demagogues with the aim of harming other people. In the Swedish school history curriculum, it is mandatory to teach students about this kind of use of history, and this book aims to address this exploitation of history for political purposes. Therefore, it might be worthwhile to take a closer look at two cases of historical revisionism that are actually closely related to each other, Holocaust denial and so-called "atrocity propaganda"; the latter will be defined later in this chapter.

I: Holocaust denial

Holocaust denial is a dangerous form of disinformation aimed at distorting history and undermining the memory of the Holocaust. By being aware of the methods used by Holocaust deniers and by applying source criticism and critical thinking, their false claims can be exposed, and historical truth defended. It is the duty of all people to honour the memory of the victims and prevent the horrific truth of the Holocaust from being questioned. The Holocaust, the systematic destruction of over six million Jews and millions of other innocent people during World War II, is one of the most well-documented historical events. Despite this, there is a small but persistent group of people who try to deny or distort the Holocaust. Their aim is to spread disinformation and undermine history's most terrible crimes against humanity.

The methods they use are diametrically opposed to the principles on which this book is based. Holocaust Denial falsely invokes source criticism, but in fact uses the opposite.

---

[*] In Israel, however, there is a different, specific content to what they call the revisionists, namely those historians who, in the 1980s, when the state archives began releasing documents on the 1948-49 war after 30 years, challenged the common narrative that no expulsion of the Palestinians ever took place because it was the Arab leaders who had urged the Palestinians to leave. Simha Faplan, Benny Morris, Ilan Pappé, Avi Shlaim and others published books that convincingly show that it was the Jewish militias Haganah – which became the IDF – as well as the Irgun and Lehi that carried out brutal massacres and expelled the people and that this was part of a deliberate and systematic plan to conquer as much land as possible with as much indigenous population as possible.

In addition, the right wing of Zionism is called "revisionism". It was founded by Ze'ev Jabotinsky in the 1920s. The Likud Party (Netanyahu's party) is the inheritor of the secular Zionist revisionism.

The Jewish Virtual Library states in its article on Holocaust denial that Holocaust deniers are characterized above all by "rejecting the personal testimony of each individual former concentration camp prisoner as unreliable".[203] This is the opposite of the present book, which focuses on the testimony of the Israeli civilians who suffered the violence of October 7, 2023.

The testimony of Holocaust victims is corroborated on a massive scale by an overwhelming amount of concrete evidence in the form of documents and testimony from the perpetrators themselves. Even these are rejected, contrary to basic source criticism, by Holocaust deniers. Source criticism teaches us to be sceptical of claims made by one side in a conflict if they paint a negative picture of the other side, but if spokespersons from one side express things that are unfavourable to the image of that side, it obviously has much more credibility.

Furthermore, Holocaust deniers use the same dishonest methods used by another form of historical revisionism and atrocity propaganda:

Hate speech: They often use hateful or offensive terms to dehumanize the group of people against whom they direct their antipathy.

Secondary sources: They use secondary sources, such as representatives of their own side who falsely "report" what alleged witnesses have said.

Selective quoting: They use quotes from people who fall under the source-critical criteria by their bias.

Falsified documents and photographs: They use falsified documents or images. This includes manipulating or editing existing images. They often take events out of context. By disregarding the broader context, they can give a false picture of historical events. An example of this is the false claim by the Nazis that they "defended themselves" against the Jews "because they declared war on Germany", which is both a conspiracy theory and an attempt to deny the chronology of Nazi antisemitism.[204]

Holocaust deniers can easily be exposed by using source criticism.

II: Atrocity propaganda

Atrocity propaganda is from a linguistic perspective the diametric opposite of Holocaust denial but is based on the same principles and actually goes hand in hand with Holocaust denial.

During World War I, atrocity propaganda was used by both the British and the French to create disgust and hatred towards German troops invading Belgium. One of the most famous and talked about events was the description of German atrocities against the civilian population in Belgium. Here are some concrete examples of atrocity propaganda used:

1. The "baby nailed to a door" story: it was claimed that German soldiers had nailed an infant to a door in a Belgian village. This story was false and was used to portray German soldiers as bestial.

2. Depictions of German atrocities against civilians: The atrocity propaganda also included false claims of rape, murder and looting by German troops in Belgian towns and villages. The aim was to create an image of German soldiers as barbaric and cruel.

3. The use of terrifying illustrations: posters and newspaper illustrations often showed dead Belgian civilians allegedly attacked by Germans, even though this was not the case.

4. Allegations of massacres of Belgian civilians: Propaganda material contained the most horrific claims that German soldiers had carried out massacres of innocent Belgian civilians, including women and children. These claims were often based on exaggerations or were simply false.

5. Depictions of destroyed towns and villages: Atrocity propaganda often used images and descriptions of destroyed Belgian towns and villages, which were used to portray German troops as destroyers and looters, even though the destruction was the result of fighting.

We should not confuse World War I Germany with the barbaric Nazi Germany. Certainly, there were cases of undisciplined German soldiers abusing Belgian civilians in the First World War – but no more so than soldiers of any nationality do in any war; of course, one cannot expect an entire male population to become law-abiding simply by wearing a uniform. What matters is whether it is an imposed policy and whether the abuses are systematic – as was the case, for example, with the German army in Poland in 1939. This was not the case with the German army in Belgium during the First World War 1914-1918, but this is what the Western Allies tried to portray through their atrocity propaganda.

Two recurring themes in atrocity propaganda throughout history are the mutilation of babies and rape. This is described in an article in The Business Standard: "The use of children in propaganda to vilify and demonize the enemy is a historical phenomenon."[205] The Business Standard gives several examples of this:

- During the Irish Catholic rebellion against British rule in Ireland in 1641, the English spread a variety of unsubstantiated stories about how "the Catholics ripped open the stomachs of pregnant women and pulled out their babies and beat them against rocks".

- The Serbian photographer who during the Yugoslav war claimed to have seen the mutilated bodies of 41 children slaughtered by Croatian National Guardsmen. This was reported all over the world, despite the lack of concrete evidence. Much later, the Serbian photographer admitted that he fabricated the whole story and his alleged eyewitnesses.

- The well-known "testimony" in October 1990 of Nayirah, a Kuwaiti teenage girl who claimed to be a nurse and that she had seen Iraqi soldiers ripping Kuwaiti babies out of incubators and throwing them on the floor. This was published in the Swedish media, among others. It was later revealed that Nayirah was the daughter of Kuwait's ambassador to the US, Saud Nasser al-Sabah. She had been coached by the PR firm Hill & Knowlton, which worked for the Kuwaiti government. Her claims were refuted by Amnesty International and others.

No group of people in history has been subjected to so much systematic atrocity propaganda as the Jews; for 1700 years the Christian church and its political followers have spread the most horrific atrocity propaganda against the Jews. Alleged abuse of children and Christian (later "Aryan") women has been central to this. "For example, 'blood libel' – the false claim that Jews use the blood of non-Jewish, usually Christian, children for ritual purposes – was widely used to persecute Jews."[206]

Rape myths also play an important role in particularly racist horror propaganda. The suppression of African Americans after the North American Civil War relied primarily on claims of alleged rape of "white" women by African Americans. These accusations were behind most of the many thousands of lynchings of African Americans in the United States.

Another example is how Britain fabricated and exaggerated reports of Indian insurgents raping 'white' women during various Indian freedom uprisings against British colonialism. These stories "also helped to justify Britain's brutal suppression of the 1857 uprisings and continued domination of India".

Allegations of rape of "Aryan" women and girls by Jewish men also played a central role in Nazi atrocity propaganda against Jews. German newspapers in the 1930s were filled with the most horrific stories of how Jews "violated Aryan girls". All this gruesome propaganda was used to justify the attacks on the Jews.

In the Swedish daily *Svenska Dagbladet* on October 9, 2020, Patrik Paulov and Per Shapiro address the topic of atrocity propaganda in the light of the Syrian conflict in our time. They quote the acclaimed British journalist Patrick Cockburn: "War always creates false stories about atrocities – alongside real atrocities. But in the case of Syria, fabricated news and one-sided reporting have taken over the news agenda in a way we probably haven't seen since the First World War." They continue: "The main problem, Cockburn argues, is that the media has uncritically accepted one side of the war, the opposition and the armed groups, as the purveyor of facts. The same side supported by public relations firms with state sponsors."[207]

Returning to the atrocity propaganda of the First World War, this kind of hate propaganda also occurred on the other side. For example, Austrian newspapers reported that 'the Serbian soldiers had a real penchant for gouging out the eyes of the Austrian wounded'. After the war, the Austrian Carl Brockhausen exposed these reports as atrocity propaganda by visiting several hospitals, without being able to find any victims of such mutilation. Carl Brockhausen therefore took the initiative to found the Internationale Rundschau to combat "systematic and thoughtless incitement of the people" – an initiative that should certainly be followed in our time.

Appendix IV
The basis of this book: source criticism

Conflicts such as the one between Israel and the Palestinian Hamas have always been complex and sensitive and attracted international attention. In an era where news and information are disseminated quickly and easily, it is particularly important to develop and use source criticism skills to understand the different perspectives and nuances of such conflicts. Source criticism is crucial in interpreting the flow of information from each such conflict and forming a clearer picture of reality. Unfortunately, Western media, not least in Sweden, have often been characterized by a virtual absence of source criticism when it comes to the conflict between Israel and Palestinian Hamas. Several examples of this have been presented in the pages of this book.

The basics of source criticism are – here based on the conflict at hand:

Diversity of Sources: Information about the conflict comes from a variety of sources, including news media, social media, political organizations, and individual commentators. The diversity of perspectives makes it even more important to assess the credibility of sources.

Agenda and Bias: Both Israeli and Palestinian sides have their own agendas and biases in the conflict. It is important to be aware of these and how they can affect the objectivity of information.

Distorted Information: Due to the passionate nature of the conflict, it is common for information to be distorted or exaggerated by different stakeholders. Source criticism helps us to distinguish truth from disinformation.

We must always use this:

The tendency criterion: which assesses the author's interest in influencing public opinion in a certain direction. This also includes the selection criterion, which assesses the author's choice of sources and their tendency, including an assessment of the missing sources that could potentially change the statement.

Here are some guidelines for applying source criticism in the context of the conflict between Israel and Hamas:

Diverse News Sources: Get news from different sources and different perspectives. This gives a more nuanced picture of the events and reduces the risk of one-sided information. Concluding that something is true just because it was claimed in "respectable" media such as *The New York Times* is the opposite of source criticism, which is always based on self-examination of what is claimed.

Verify the facts: Double-check claims with multiple sources.

Check the Background of the Source: Try to understand the background of news or information sources. Who are they? What are their purposes and interests in the conflict? Always be sceptical of claims made by one side in a conflict, especially if they portray the other side negatively.

Be sceptical of pictures and videos: pictures and videos can be easily manipulated. Be careful about accepting images as proof of events and try to find confirmation from other sources.

Contextualize: Try to put the information in a broader context. What happened before and after the incident? What factors may have influenced the situation?

Falsify: Assess your own bias: Take your own bias into account so that you are not misled by your own feelings and prejudices.

The philosopher of science Karl Popper talked about something he called falsification, that when you have a thesis, you should not look for things that confirm it – it is not difficult; even the Bible says "Seek and you shall find" – but for things that can disprove it. It is only when you have not been able to find any valid arguments against your thesis that you can accept it. This principle has guided every conclusion presented in this book.

Notes

1 Alice Speri, *"Beheaded Babies" Report Spread Wide and Fast – but Israel Military Won't Confirm It.* https://theintercept.com/2023/10/11/israel-hamas-disinformation/, October 11, 2023.

2 Amos Harel, *Failures Leading Up to the Hamas Attack That Changed Israel Forever*, Haaretz, 2023-10-20, https://www.haaretz.com/israel-news/2023-10-20/ty-article/.premium/underprepared-and-overconfident-israel-failed-to-spot-the-signs-of-impending-disaster/0000018b-4976-d03a-afcb-697edb020000.

3 Miko Peled, *The General's Son - Journey of an Israeli in Palestine*, Just World Books, 2016; Bengt Hermele, *Judejävel*, Leopard förlag, 2016.

4 Menachem Begin, *The Revolt*, 1951

5 *Albert Einstein Letter to The New York Times. December 4, 1948 New Palestine Party. Visit of Menachen Begin and Aims of Political Movement Discussed*, https://archive.org/details/AlbertEinstein-LetterToTheNewYorkTimes.December41948

6 Göran Burén, *Mordet på Folke Bernadotte*, Leopard förlag, Stockholm, 2012.

7 Ronen Bergman, *Rise and kill first. The secret history of Israel's targeted assassinations*, John Murray Publishers Carmelite House, 2018.

8 Jonathan Glancey, *Our last occupation, Gas, chemicals, bombs: Britain has used them all before in Iraq*, The Guardian, 2003-04-19, https://www.theguardian.com/world/2003/apr/19/iraq.arts

9 Amnesty International, *Israel: Palestinian armed groups must be held accountable for deliberate civilian killings, abductions and indiscriminate attacks*, 2023-10-12, https://www.amnesty.org/en/latest/news/2023/10/israel-palestinian-armed-groups-must-be-held-accountable-for-deliberate-civilian-killings-abductions-and-indiscriminate-attacks/

Human Rights Watch, *Israel/Palestine: Videos of* Hamas-*Led Attacks Verified*, 2023-10-18, https://www.hrw.org/news/2023/10/18/israel/palestine-videos-hamas-led-attacks-verified

10 Adam Shatz, *Vengeful Pathologies*, London Review of Books, Vol. 45, no. 21, 2023-11-02, https://www.lrb.co.uk/the-paper/v45/n21/adam-shatz/vengeful-pathologies

11 Juliet Samuel, *Why is the UK tiptoeing around hate merchants?* The Times, 2023-10-11, https://www.thetimes.co.uk/article/why-is-the-uk-tiptoeing-around-hate-merchants-fh0jfcnkf

12 *SD-ledaren: Utvisa de som firar* Hamasattacker, 2023-10-10, https://sverigesradio.se/artikel/sd-ledaren-utvisa-de-som-firar-hamas-attacker

13 Iftikhar Gilani, *'This was an act of resistance against the occupation army': Hanan Ashrawi*, 2023-10-30, https://frontline.thehindu.com/world-affairs/hanan-ashrawi-spokesperson-for-plo-interview-on-palestine-hamas-attack/article67465345.ece

14 Norman Finkelstein, *Nat Turner in Gaza*, 26 Oct 2023, https://normanfinkelstein.substack.com/p/nat-turner-in-gaza

15 *They are worse than ISIS': Israel PM Netanyahu's call with US President Biden on* Hamas, The Print, 2023-10-11, https://www.youtube.com/watch?v=BjrFId0uM3I

16 Babi Yar is a ravine on the western outskirts of Kiev, Ukraine. The ravine was the site of several mass executions during World War II. The first and best documented took place on September 29-30, 1941, when 33 771 Ukrainian Jews were shot dead by the Nazi Einsatzgruppen. In total, more than 100,000 people are estimated to have been murdered in Babi Yar during the war. Wikipedia https://www.wikiwand.com/sv/Babi_Yar

17 By Matthew Chance, Richard Allen Greene and Joshua Berlinger, *Israeli official says government cannot confirm babies were beheaded in Hamas attack*, CNN, https://edition.cnn.com/2023/10/12/middleeast/israel-hamas-beheading-claims-intl/index.html

18 Owen Jones, *I Watched The Hamas Massacre Film. Here Are My Thoughts*, 2023-11-27, https://www.youtube.com/watch?v=mc5iG3DX7ho

19 *Hasbara Handbook: Promoting Israel on Campus, The World Union of Jewish Students*, 2002, http://www.middle-east-info.org/take/wujshasbara.pdf, page 8

20 *A growing number of reports indicate Israeli forces responsible for Israeli civilian and military deaths following October 7 attack*, Mondoweiss, 22 October 2023, https://mondoweiss.net/2023/10/a-growing-number-of-reportsindicate-israeli-forcesresponsible-for-israeli-civilian-and-military-deaths-following-october-7-attack/

21 *An open letter to Israelis from Israelis: We deserve the truth about October 7*, Mondoweiss, 2023-10-31 https://mondoweiss.net/2023/10/an-open-letter-to-israelis-from-israelis-we-deserve-the-truth-about-october-7/

22 https://twitter.com/IsraelMFA/status/1712330627607924776

23 Sagi Cohen, *Conspiracy Theories and Lies | Denial of Hamas' October 7 Massacre Is Gaining Pace Online*, Haaretz, 2023-11-07, https://www.haaretz.com/israel-news/2023-11-07/ty-article/.premium/denial-of-hamas-october-7-massacre-is-gaining-pace-online/0000018b-aa45-d5aa-a19f-afffabf10000

24 Nir Hasson, Liza Rozovsky, *Hamas committed documented atrocities. But a few false stories feed the deniers*, Haaretz, 2023-12-04, https://www.haaretz.com/israel-news/2023-12-04/ty-article-magazine/.premium/hamas-committed-documented-atrocities-but-a-few-false-stories-feed-the-deniers/0000018c-34f3-da74-afce-b5fbe24f0000

25 *WATCH NOW: BEHEADED BABIES AND WOMEN FOUND IN KFAR AZA*, i24News, live 2023-10-10, https://www.youtube.com/watch?v=RKc9ESIEMpw

26 An article in *The Times of Israel* shows somehow different figures – it is difficult to assess how this and other newspapers have arrived at the figures they report. *14 kids under 10, 25 people over 80: Up-to-date breakdown of Oct 7 victims we know about, The Times of Israel*, 2023-12-04, https://www.timesofisrael.com/14-kids-under-10-25-people-over-80-up-to-date-breakdown-of-oct-7-victims-we-know-about/

27 *Remarks by President Biden at a Campaign Reception*, The White House, 2023-12-12, https://www.whitehouse.gov/briefing-room/speeches-remarks/2023/12/12/remarks-by-president-biden-at-a-campaign-reception-5/

28 Alice Speri, *"Beheaded Babies" Report Spread Wide and Fast — but Israel Military Won't Confirm It*, https://theintercept.com/2023/10/11/israel-hamas-disinformation/, October 11 2023.

29 Yaniv Kubovich, *Graphic Videos and Incitement: How the IDF Misleads Israelis on Telegram*, Haaretz, December 12, 2023, https://www.haaretz.com/israel-news/security-aviation/2023-12-12/ty-article/.premium/graphic-videos-and-incitement-how-the-idf-is-misleading-israelis-on-telegram/0000018c-5ab5-df2f-adac-febd01c30000

30 Yaniv Kubovich, *"Israeli Army Admits Running Unauthorized Graphic Gaza Influence Op"*, Haaretz, February 2, 2024, https://www.haaretz.com/israel-news/security-aviation/2024-02-04/ty-article/.premium/israeli-army-its-admits-staff-was-behind-graphic-gaza-telegram-channel/0000018d-70b4-dd6e-a98d-f4b6a9c00000

31 International Committee of the Red Cross (ICRC), *The Geneva Conventions of 12 August 1949*, Geneva, Switzerland.

32 ICRC, ibid, page 31.

33 2004-01-04, *Israel's Dead: The Names of Those Killed in Hamas Attacks, Massacres and the Israel-Hamas War*, https://www.haaretz.com/haaretz-explains/2023-10-19/ty-article-magazine/ israels-dead-the-names-of-those-killed-in-hamas-massacres-and-the-israel-hamas-war/ 0000018b-325c-d450-a3af-7b5cf0210000.

Linda Dayan and Maya Lecker, *How Haaretz Is Counting Israel's Dead From the October 7 Hamas Attack*, Haaretz, 2023-11-23 hhttps://www.haaretz.com/haaretz-explains/2023-11-23/ty-article-magazine/.premium/how-haaretz-is-counting-israels-dead-from-the-october-7-hamas-attack/0000018b-d42c-d423 affb-f7afe1a70000

34 Gershon Shafir, *Land, Labor and the Origins of the Israeli-Palestinian Conflict, 1882-1914*, University of California Press, Berkely and Los Angeles, 1996, page 188.

35 Ido Efrati, Yanich Kubovich, *IDF reports 1,593 wounded since October 7, but hospital data is much higher*, Haaretz 2023-12-10, https://www.haaretz.com/israel-news/2023-12-10/ty-article/.premium/idf-reports-1-593-wounded-since-october-7-but-hospital-data-is-much-higher/0000018c-552ddf4b- a78e-d52f47ac0000.

36 Yair Assulim, *The 'Accidental' Execution of a Civilian Must Be a Reminder: Immorality kills*, Haaretz, 2023-12-07, https://www.haaretz.com/opinion/2023-12-07/ty-article-opinion/.premium/the-accidental- execution-of-a-civilian-must-be-a-reminder-immorality-kills/0000018c-45cf-db80-afbd-cfffc0f30000

37 Tamar Michaelis, Richard Allen Greene and Joshua Berlinger, *What we know about how 3 Israeli hostages were killed by the IDF*, CNN, 2023-12-20, https://edition.cnn.com/2023/12/16/middleeast/what-we-know-hostages-killed-israel-gaza/index.html

38 Yoav Zitun, *One-fifth of troop fatalities in Gaza due to friendly fire or accidents*, IDF reports, Ynet, 2023-12-12, https://www.ynetnews.com/article/rkjqoobip

39 Amos Harel, *Failures Leading Up to the Hamas Attack That Changed Israel forever*, Haaretz, 2023-10-20, https://www.haaretz.com/israel-news/2023-10-20/ty-article/.premium/underprepared-andoverconfident- israel-failed-to-spot-the-signs-of-impending-disaster/0000018b-4976-d03a-afcb- 697edb020000

40 Civil Administration is the common name of the Coordinator of Government Activities in the Territories (COGAT), a unit of the IDF that coordinates civil affairs between the Government of Israel, the IDF, international organizations, diplomats, and the Palestinian Authority. It is the main body remaining of the largely defunct Israeli Civil Administration that governed the West Bank and Gaza Strip between 1981 and 1994 (Wikipedia).

41 *'That was a mistake': Mehdi challenges Israeli adviser Mark Regev on false Israeli claims*, MSNBC, 2023-11-16, https://www.youtube.com/watch?v=HD-yRuTasHU. Quoted and commented on Electronic Intifada: *Ali Abunimah, Israel admits burning hundreds of people on 7 October*, https://electronicintifada.net/ blogs/ali-abunimah/israel-admits-burning-hundreds-people-7-october

42 https://videoidf.azureedge.net/95779766-cd51-48dc-808d-5330a041c1e6

43 X (Twitter) https://twitter.com/IsraelMFA/status/1712330627607924776

44 Bill Hutchinson, *Israel's 'Ground Zero:' The Be'eri Kibbutz was among the bloodiest scenes of the Hamas attack*, ABC News, 2023-10-13, https://abcnews.go.com/International/israels-ground-zero-Be'eri-kibbutz-bloodiest-scenes-hamas/story?id=103936668

45 Ali Abunimah and David Sheen, *Israeli general killed Israelis on 7 October then lied about it*, 2023- 12-24, https://electronicintifada.net/content/israeli-general-killed-israelis-7-october-then-lied-about-it/43176. There are several embedded videos in the article. The interview with General Barak Hiram is the third, right at the bottom of the page.

46 The interview in Hebrew can be found on the Radio Kans website: https://www.kan.org.il/content/kan/ kan-b/p-9969/#. The full interview written in English can be found below the article on the Electronic Intifada:

Ali Abunimah and David Sheen, *Israeli forces shot their own civilians, kibbutz survivor says*, Electronic Intifada, October 16, 2023, https://electronicintifada.net/content/israeli-forces-shot-their-own-civilians-kibbutz-survivor-says/38861.

47 https://www.mako.co.il/news-military/6361323ddea5a810/Article-f5fdaeb7aeb4c81027.htm

48 See note 44.

49 Quoted in Ali Abunimah and David Sheen, *Israeli forces shot their own civilians, kibbutz survivor says*, Electronic Intifada, October 16, 2023, see note 45.
Nir Hasson (only in Hebrew), https://www.haaretz.co.il/news/politics/2023-10-20/ty-article-magazine/.premium/0000018b-499a-dc3c-a5df-ddbaab290000?fbclid= IwAR1bObZUau2KRdE-vOvGqskFyVLkVxknDg7dHm9dfgsbUbi8ECFJQZYri0As

50 Quique Kierszenbaum, *'It was a pogrom': Be'eri survivors on the horrific attack by Hamas terrorists*, The Guardian, 2023-10-11, https://www.theguardian.com/world/2023/oct/11/it-was-a-pogrom-Be'eri-survivors-horrific-attack-hamas-terrorists

51 *Military veteran recounts Israeli helicopter firing missiles in kibbutz Be'eri*, Middle East Eye, 2023-12-15, https://www.youtube.com/watch?v=PFxrl8nUb7Q

52 https://www.mako.co.il/news-military/6361323ddea5a810/Article-5de7f6883ef7c81026.htm Translated to English: Ali Abunimah and David Sheen, *Israeli general killed Israelis on 7 October then lied about it*, The Electronic Intifada, 2023-12-24, https://electronicintifada.net/content/ israeli-general-killed-israelis-7-october-then-lied-about-it/43176

53 Neftali Bennet on X (Twitter). https://twitter.com/naftalibennett/status/1724419046123164135

54 Ali Abunimah and David Sheen, *Israeli child "burned completely" by Israeli tank fire at kibbutz*, 2023-11-25, https://electronicintifada.net/content/israeli-child-burned-completely-israeli-tankfire-kibbutz/41706. Radiointervjun på hebreiska: https://rephonic.com/episodes/t2oyo-klmnlybrmn-kalman-liberman-151123-hyvm-h-40.

55 *Female IDF soldiers recount tank battle on October 7*, 2023-11-28, #i24NEWSDesk, https://www.youtube.com/watch?v=oA9RLwInqn4

56 *Senior retired US government official speaks out on Gaza*, 2024-01-07, https://www.jewishvoiceforlabour.org.uk/article/senior-retired-us-government-official-speaks-out-on-gaza/

57 https://www.youtube.com/watch?v=8-jhoAs_O-g

58 *A growing number of reports indicate Israeli forces responsible for Israeli civilian and military deaths following October 7 attack*, Mondoweiss, 2023-10-22, https://mondoweiss.net/2023/10/a-growing-number-of-reports-indicate-israeli-forces-responsible-for-israeli-civilian-and-military-deaths-following-october-7-attack/

59 Amnesty International, *Gaza 'Black Friday': Cutting edge investigation points to Israeli war crimes*, https://www.amnesty.org/en/latest/news/2015/07/gaza-cutting-edge-investigation-rafah/
United Nations, Human Rights Council, *The United Nations Independent Commission of Inquiry on the 2014 Gaza Conflict*, https://www.ohchr.org/en/hr-bodies/hrc/co-i-gaza-conflict/reportco-in-gaza

60 https://www.wikiwand.com/en/Hannibal_Directive

61 Adam Shatz, *Israel's Putinisation*, London Review of Books, Vol. 38 No. 4 · 18 February 2016 https://www.lrb.co.uk/the-paper/v38/n04/adam-shatz/israel-s-putinisation

62 Rachel Fink, *'Unlawful, Unethical, Horrifying': IDF Ethics Code Author on Alleged Use of 'Hannibal Directive' During Hamas Attack*, January 17, 2024, https://www.haaretz.com/israel-news/2024-01-17/ty-article/.premium/unlawful-unethical-horrifying-idf-ethics-expert-on-controversial-hannibal-directive/0000018d-186c-dd75-addd-faedd2b80000

63 *Hannibal Protocol – Endangering the Lives of Soldiers and Civilians*, Feruary 15, 2015 https://law.acri.org.il/en/2015/02/15/hannibal-protocol/

64 Ali Abunimah, *"Shoot at everything": How Israeli pilots killed their own civilians*, 2023-11-11. https://electronicintifada.net/blogs/ali-abunimah/shoot-everything-how-israeli-pilots-killed-their-own-civilians
This is a long article with several embedded videos. The first is from the IDF and is filmed from inside a helicopter. At the bottom of the page David Sheen has translated Yoav Zitun's article.

65 Yoav Zitun, *Hamas deception of IDF helicopters and directing pilots on WhatsApp – Airforce on the 1st*, only in the Hebrew edition, Ynet, 2023-10-15, https://www.ynet.co.il/news/article/b111niukzt

66 Legacy Special Report on Israel vs HAMAS Legacy Conversations, *We spoke to Major Graeme Ipp (Israeli Army Rtd)*, 2023-11-14, https://www.youtube.com/watch?v=HOsv-qI8c-c

67 *Israel Police slams 'Haaretz' claim IDF helicopter may have harmed civilians on Oct. 7*, The Times of Israel, 2023-11-23, https://www.timesofisrael.com/liveblog_entry/israel-police-slams-haaretzclaim-idf-helicopter-may-have-harmed-civilians-on-oct-7/

68 Josh Breiner, *Israeli Security Establishment: Hamas Likely Didn't Have Advance Knowledge of Nova Festival*, Haaretz, 2023-11-18, https://www.haaretz.com/israel-news/2023-11-18/ty-article/.premium/israeli-security-establishment-hamas-likely-didnt-have-prior-knowledge-of-nova-festival/0000018b-e2ee-d168-a3ef-f7fe8ca20000

69 Asa Winstanley, *We blew up Israeli houses on 7 October, says Israeli colonel*, Electronic Intifada, 2023-12-05, https://electronicintifada.net/blogs/asa-winstanley/we-blew-israeli-houses-7-october-says-israeli-colonel

The Hebrew interview can be retrieved on Haaretz podcast "The Week": https://www.haaretz.co.il/digital/ podcast/weekly/2023-11-09/ty-article-podcast/0000018b-b3a5-d3c1-a39b-bfe55acb0000

70 Noa Limone, *If Israel Used a Controversial Procedure Against Its Citizens, We Need to Talk About It Now*, Haaretz, 2023-12-13, https://www.haaretz.com/opinion/2023-12-13/ty-article-opinion/.premium/if-israel-used-a-procedure-against-its-citizens-we-need-to-talk-about-it-now/0000018c-6383-de43-affd-f783212e0000

71 Maya Lecker, *I Want to Believe the IDF Won't Shoot Unarmed Civilians Holding a White Flag*, 2023- 12-17, https://www.haaretz.com/israel-news/haaretz-today/2023-12-17/ty-article/.highlight/i-want-to-believe-the-idf-wont-shoot-unarmed-civilians-holding-a-white-flag/0000018c-7896-d301-a3ac-fed78b050000 64

72 *Video: Soldier executes Palestinian lying injured on ground after the latter stabbed a soldier in Hebron*, B'tselem, 2016-03-24, https://www.btselem.org/video/20160324_soldier_executes_palestinian_attacker_in_hebron#full

73 B'tselem is an Israeli organization that monitors human rights in the occupied territories. They have a program that involves distributing video cameras to Palestinians in the West Bank who use them for documenting human rights abuses.

74 *Elor Azaria: From killer to 'king' – leading life of luxury in Israel*, Middle East Eye, 2018-08-29, https://www.middleeasteye.net/news/elor-azaria-killer-king-leading-life-luxury-israel

75 Jessica Steinberg, *Survivors share accounts of encounters with terrorists, and an escape from Gaza*, The Times of Israel, 2023-10-09, https://www.timesofisrael.com/survivors-share-harrowingaccounts- saving-kids-and-a-courageous-escape-from-gaza/

76 *Israeli woman speaks of experience with Hamas fighters*, Middle East Eye, 2023-10-10, https://www.youtube.com/watch?v=rD7NI0tGbp8

77 *Lifshitz press conference panned as disastrous for Israel, PR win for* Hamas, 2023-10-24, The Times of Israel, https://www.timesofisrael.com/liveblog_entry/lifshitz-press-conference-panned-asdisastrous- for-israel-pr-win-for-hamas/

78 *Israeli hostage Yarden Roman-Gat shares details of her captivity in Gaza*, 60 Minutes, https://www.youtube.com/watch?v=ixynqr-88gE

79 Interview with Channel 12 published on Middle East Eye, 20223-12-25, https://www.youtube.com/watch?v=ZIMfc1y59mM

80 Mira Fox, *Debate rages over whether a letter from an Israeli hostage to her Hamas captors is a fake. But does it matter?* 2023-11-30, Forward, https://forward.com/culture/571714/hostage-letter-danielle-aloni-hamas-morality/

81 Patrick Kingsley, *'I Left Him Behind': Freed Hostage Fears for Father, Still in Gaza*, 2023-12-21, The New York Times, https://www.nytimes.com/2023/12/21/world/middleeast/hamas-israel-father-hostage.html

82 Jeffrey Gettleman, Anat Schwartz and Adam Sella, *'Screams Without Words': How Hamas Weaponized Sexual Violence on Oct. 7*, The New York Times, 2023-12-28, https://www.nytimes.com/2023/12/28/world/middleeast/oct-7-attacks-hamas-israel-sexual-violence.html

83 *Family of key case in New York Times October 7 sexual violence report renounces story, says reporters manipulated them*, Mondoweiss, 2024-01-03. https://mondoweiss.net/2024/01/family-of-key-case-in-new-york-times-october-7-sexual-violence- report-renounces-story-says-reporters-manipulated-them/

84 Ali Abunimah, *Watch: NY Times "investigation" of mass rape by Hamas falls apart*, The Electronic Intifada, 2024-01-09, https://electronicintifada.net/blogs/ali-abunimah/watch-ny-timesinvestigation- mass-rape-hamas-falls-apart

85 https://www.aljazeera.com/program/the-listening-post/2024/3/2/the-unraveling-of-the-new-york-times-hamas-rape-story

86 Nir Hasson and Liza Rozovsky, *Hamas committed documented atrocities. But a few false stories feed the deniers*, Haaretz, 2023 -12-04

87 Liza Rozovsky and Josh Breiner, *'It Takes Strength to Speak Out' | Israeli Police Ask Victims and Witnesses to Testify About Hamas Sexual Violence*, Haaretz, 2024-01-04, https://www.haaretz.com/israel-news/2024-01-04/ty-article/.premium/israeli-police-ask-victims-and-witnesses-to-testify-about-hamas-sexual-violence/0000018c-d580-d751-ad8d-ffa4acf40000

88 Judith Levine, *There Was No Cover-Up of* Hamas's *Sexual Violence on October 7*, The Intercept, 2023-12-24, https://theintercept.com/2023/12/24/feminism-sexual-violence-hamas-israel/

89 Bethan McKernan, *Israel women's groups warn of failure to keep evidence of sexual violence in Hamas attacks*, The Guardian, 2023-11-10, https://www.theguardian.com/world/2023/nov/10/israel-womens-groups-warn-of-failure-to-keep-evidence-of-sexual-violence-in-hamas-attacks

90 Hilo Glazer, *The Scope of* Hamas' *Campaign of Rape Against Israeli Women Is Revealed, Testimony After Testimony*, Haaretz, 2023-11-30, https://www.haaretz.com/israel-news/2023-11-30/ty-articlemagazine/. highlight/hamas-campaign-of-rape-against-israeli-women-is-revealed-testimony-aftertestimony/ 0000018c-2144-da36-a1de-6767dac90000

91 Physicians for Human Rights, *Position Paper, Sexual and Gender Based and Sexual Violence as a Weapon of War During the 7 October Attacks*, November 2023

92 https://www.youtube.com/watch?v=5D7tb4zFKdk&ab_channel=MaimonidesSocietyHarvard-MedicalSchoolandHSDM

93 The Times of Israel, *IDF taps chief rabbi who once seemed to permit wartime rape*, 2016-07-12, https://www.timesofisrael.com/idf-taps-chief-rabbi-who-once-seemed-to-permit-wartime-rape/

94 https://www.gov.il/BlobFolder/news/arcci-submits-first-report-to-un-21-feb-2024/en/English_Swords_of_Iron_DOCUMENTS_Sexual%20violence%20crimes%20on%20Ocober%207-Feb.%202024.pdf

95 https://www.un.org/sexualviolenceinconflict/mission-report-official-visit-of-the-office-of-the-srsg-svc-to-israel-and-the-occupied-west-bank-29-january-14-february-2024/

96 The Times of Israel, *UN official in Israel asks victims of Hamas sexual assault to 'break silence'*, 2024-01-30, https://www.timesofisrael.com/un-official-in-israel-asks-victims-of-hamas-sexual-assault-to-break-silence/

97 Liza Rozovsky and Josh Breiner, 'It Takes Strength to Speak Out' | Israeli Police Ask Victims and Witnesses to Testify About Hamas Sexual Violence [Artikelrubriken kursiv], 2024-01-04, Haaretz, https://www.haaretz.com/israel-news/2024-01-04/ty-article/.premium/israeli-police-ask-victims-and-witnesses-to-testify-about-hamas-sexual-violence/0000018c-d580-d751-ad8d-ffa4acf40000

98 See note 43.

99 Jeremy Scahill, Ryan Grim, *Kibbutz Be'eri Rejects Story in New York Times October 7 Exposé: "They Were Not Sexually Abused"*, The Intercept, March 4 2024,

100 https://www.youtube.com/watch?v=Q_ttE9_1stM

101 Arun Gupta, *American Media Keep Citing Zaka — Though Its October 7 Atrocity Stories Are Discredited in Israel - Israeli media has debunked the ultra-Orthodox group's stories, but the New York Times won't say so*, The Intercept, 2024-02-27, https://theintercept.com/2024/02/27/zaka-october-7-israel-hamas-new-york-times/

102 Sheera Frenkel, *They Thought They Knew Death, but That Didn't Prepare Them for Oct. 7*, The New York Times, 2024-01-15

103 Liza Rozovsky and Josh Breiner, *Israeli Army Officer Makes Incorrect Claims on October 7 Massacre; IDF: 'We'll Set the Record Straight'*, Haaretz, 2024-01-21

104 Nic Robertson, *"Evidence suggests gunmen at music festival threw grenade into bomb shelter"*, CNN, 2023-10-10. https://edition.cnn.com/middleeast/live-news/israel-hamas-war-gaza-10-10- 23/h_b1de84e5626693eb45015eff2a8c39c7

105 Anderson Cooper, *Dashcam shows Hamas gunman shooting freely during music festival attack,* CNN, https://edition.cnn.com/videos/world/2023/10/14/hamas-nova-festival-attack-site-visit-cooper-dnt-ac360-vpx.cnn

106 Josh Breiner, *Israeli Security Establishment: Hamas Likely Didn't Have Advance Knowledge of Nova Festival,* Haaretz, 2023-11-18 https://www.haaretz.com/israel-news/2023-11-18/ty-article/.premium/israeli-security-establishment-hamas-likely-didnt-have-prior-knowledge-of-nova-festival/0000018b-e2ee-d168-a3ef-f7fe8ca20000.

107 Paul P. Murphy, Teele Rebane, Hilary Whiteman, Brad Lendon, Amanda Jackson and David Williams, *Israel festival revelers shot at point-blank range,* video shows, CNN, 2023-10-10 https://edition. cnn.com/2023/10/09/middleeast/israel-hamas-music-festival-aftermath-intl-hnk/index.html

108 https://en.wikipedia.org/wiki/Kidnapping_of_Noa_Argamani

109 *Father of girl taken to Gaza says he hopes people can come together,* MiddleEastEye, 2023-10-10, https://www.middleeasteye.net/news/israel-palestine-war-father-girl-taken-gaza-hopes-come-together

110 https://edition.cnn.com/interactive/2023/10/middleeast/hamas-music-festival-attack-investigation-cmd-intl/

111 J Street, *Noam Cohen's story of survival during the horrific Hamas terror attack at the Nova music festival,* 2023-10-12, https://www.youtube.com/watch?v=bLej--SSCDA

112 https://www.tv4.se/artikel/7meWlE8yEyKKYQoYCrOt5B/i-stunden-blev-det-kaos-ingen-kangarantera- vad-som-skedde

113 Daphna Baram, *I was in Israel when Hamas attacked – now we must reflect on the senselessness of killing and being killed,* The Guardian, 2023-10-11, https://www.theguardian.com/commentis-free/2023/oct/11/israel-hamas-benjamin-netanyahu-peace

114 *WATCH NOW: BEHEADED BABIES AND WOMEN FOUND IN KFAR AZA,* 2023-10-10, https://www.youtube.com/watch?v=RKc9ESIEMpw

115 Thomas L. Friedman, *Israel Is Losing Its Greatest Asset: Acceptance,* The New York Time, Feb. 27, 2024.

116 BBC, Hard Talk, Stephen Sackur speaks to Israel's former prime minister Naftali Bennett, who is a staunch supporter of Israel's military assault in Gaza, 2023-12-20, https://www.bbc.co.uk/iplayer/episode/m001tnjh/hardtalk-naftali-bennett-former-prime-minister-of-israel

117 Adam Rasgon and David Kirkpatrick, *What Was Hamas Thinking?* 20123-10-13, The New Yorker, https://www.newyorker.com/news/news-desk/what-was-hamas-thinking

118 *Hamas pledges to release all foreign prisoners 'when field conditions allow',* 2023-10-17, The Cradle, https://new.thecradle.co/articles-id/7791

119 Summer Said, *Iran Says Hamas Is Ready to Release Hostages but Can't Do So Under Israeli Bombing,* 2023-10-18, The Wall Street Journal, https://www.wsj.com/livecoverage/israel-hamas-war-gaza-palestinians/card/iran-says-hamas-is-ready-to-release-hostages-but-can-t-do-so-under-israeli-bombing-FG7XcFDk1654SNq1mqvR

120 *Hamas says Israel refused to receive 2 hostages; Israel calls it propaganda,* 2023-11-21, https://www.aljazeera.com/news/2023/10/21/hamas-says-israel-refused-to-receive-2-hostages-israel-calls-it-propaganda

121 Adam Shatz, *Vengeful pathologies,* London Review of Books, Vol. 45 No. 21, 2023-11-02, https://www.lrb.co.uk/the-paper/v45/n21/adam-shatz/vengeful-pathologies

122 Abdaljawad Omar, *Hopeful pathologies in the war for Palestine: a reply to Adam Shatz,* Mondoweiss, 2023-11-08 https://mondoweiss.net/2023/11/hopeful-pathologies-in-the-war-for-palestine-a-reply-to-adam-shatz/

123 Ilan Pappé, *Ten Myths on Israel*, Verso, London, 2017, page 118.

124 See *Fact Sheet: Israel's E1 Settlement, Institute for Middle East UnderEsting,* IMEU, 2021-12-09, https://imeu.org/article/fact-sheet-israels-e1-settlement

125 Jonathan Freeland: *Warning: Benjamin Netanyahu is walking right into Hamas's trap,* The Guardian, 2023-10-20, https://www.theguardian.com/commentisfree/2023/oct/20/benjamin-netanyahu-hamas-israel-prime-minister

126 *Palestinian Organizations Call for Immediate Action from the International Community to Stop Israel's Reprisals against Palestinian Civilians,* 2023-10-08, https://www.mezan.org/en/post/46275/Palestinian-Organizations-Call-for-Immediate-Action-from-the-International-Community-to-Stop-Israel%E2%80%99s-Reprisals-against-Palestinian-Civilians#_ftnref1

127 Hagar Shezaf, *Six Palestinians Have Died in Israeli Prisons During the War, Two Found Bruised,* 2023-12-09, https://www.haaretz.com/israel-news/2023-12-09/ty-article-magazine/.premium/six-palestinians-have-died-in-israeli-prisons-during-the-war-two-found-bruised/0000018c-4ea8-df4b-a78e-dfab60f10000

128 Fayha Shalash, *Israel-Palestine war: Family of prisoner say he was beaten to death in Israeli jail,* Middle East Eye, 2023-10-27, https://www.middleeasteye.net/news/israel-palestine-war-family-prisoner-beaten-death-prison

129 Yoav Haifawi, *How administrative detention is used to terrorize '48 Palestinians Since October 7,* Mondoweiss, 2023-12-25, https://mondoweiss.net/2023/12/how-administrative-detentionis-used-to-terrorize-48-palestinians/

130 Human Rights Watch, *Israel: Gaza Workers Held Incommunicado for Weeks,* 2024-01-03, https://www.hrw.org/news/2024/01/03/israel-gaza-workers-held-incommunicado-weeks#:~:text=(Jerusalem)%20%E2%80%93%20Israeli%20authorities%20held,conditions%2C%20Human%20Rights%20Watch%20said.

131 Chantal Da Silva, *Nakba 2023': Israel right-wing ministers' comments add fuel to Palestinian fears,* NBC, 2023-11-13, https://www.nbcnews.com/news/world/gaza-nakba-israels-far-right-palestinian-fears-hamas-war-rcna123909

132 AP, *Israel used 'calorie count' to limit Gaza food during blockade, critics claim,* 2012-10-17 https://www.theguardian.com/world/2012/oct/17/israeli-military-calorie-limit-gaza

133 *GAZA TEN YEARS LATER, UN's Country Team in the occupied Palestinian territory,* July 2017, https://unsco.unmissions.org/gaza-ten-years-later-report-july-2017

134 Who Profits, *Captive economy, The Pharmaceutical Industry and the Israeli Occupation,* July 2012, https://www.whoprofits.org/publications/report/61?captive-economy

135 Yuval Abraham, *The hostages weren't our top priority': How Israel's bombing frenzy endangered captives in Gaza,* 2023-12-17, +972magazine, https://www.972mag.com/israel-bombing-endangered-hostages-gaza/

136 Melanie Lidman, Videos of soldiers acting maliciously in Gaza create new headache for Israel, Los Angeles Times, 2023-12-13, https://www.latimes.com/world-nation/story/2023-12-13/israelisoldiers- videos-acting-maliciously-gaza

137 Twitter, https://twitter.com/jacksonhinklle/status/1728457931136626767

138 B'tselem, *Protect civilians from the impact of hostilities,* 2023-10-27, https://www.btselem.org/press_releases/20231027_protect_civilians_from_the_impact_of_hostilities

139 Quoted in Middle East Eye, Avi Shlaim, *War on Gaza: Netanyahu, Hamas and the origins of the 2023 Nakba war,* 2023-12-21, https://www.middleeasteye.net/big-story/gaza-war-israel-netanyahu-hamas- origins-2023-nakba

140 Ze'ev Jabotinsky, *The Iron Wall,* 1923-11-04, https://en.jabotinsky.org/media/9747/the-iron-wall.pdf

141 Human Rights Watch, *Israel: Starvation Used as Weapon of War in Gaza,* 2023-12-18 https://www.hrw.org/news/2023/12/18/israel-starvation-used-weapon-war-gaza

142 *Israel counted calorie requirements of Gazans during blockade*, The Times of Israel, 2012-10-12https://www.timesofisrael.com/israel-counted-calorie-requirements-of-gazans-during-land-blockade-to-avoid-crisis/

143 *Weapons hidden in incubators in the Kamal Adwan hospital*, IDF, 2023-12-16, https://www.idf.il/en/mini-sites/hamas-israel-war-24/war-on-hamas-2023-resources/weaponshidden- in-incubators-in-the-kamal-adwan-hospital/#:~:text=IDF%20and%20ISA%20forces%20 questioned,documents%2C%20and%20tactical%20communications%20equipment.

144 Miriam Berger, Evan Hill and Hazem Balousha, *Israel's assault forced a nurse to leave babies behind. They were found decomposing*, The Washington Post, 2023-12-03, https://www.washingtonpost.com/world/2023/12/03/gaza-premature-babies-dead-nasr/

145 https://visualizingpalestine.org/visuals/checkpoint-births

146 By Louisa Loveluck, Evan Hill, Jonathan Baran, Jarrett Ley and Ellen Nakashima, *The case of al-Shifa: Investigating the assault on Gaza's largest hospital*, The Washington Post, 2023- 12-21, https://www.washingtonpost.com/world/2023/12/21/al-shifa-hospital-gaza-hamas-israel/

147 Saada Allaw, Nour Kelzi, *Ghassan Abu Sitta: Genocide in Gaza*, 2024-01-29, https://english.legal-agenda.com/ghassan-abu-sitta-genocide-in-gaza/#:~:text=Having%20 spent%2043%20days%20amidst,is%20being%20waged%20on%20Gaza.

148 Natasha Roth-Rowland, *When never again becomes a war cry*, 2023-10-28, +972 magazine, https://www.972mag.com/never-again-gaza-war-holocaust/

149 However, it was not evident that the Partition Plan would be adopted. The vote in the General Assembly was: 33 in favor, 13 against, 10 abstaining, and one absent. Several countries complained that they had been subjected to various pressures from the Zionists and the US, such as offers of bribes and threats to cut aid. There is a rich literature on this. See Wikipedia, *United Nations Partition Plan for Palestine*, section The vote. https://www.wikiwand.com/en/United_Nations_Partition_Plan_for_Palestine#Reports_of_pressure_for_and_against_the_Plan

150 Quoted in Menachem Begin, The Revolt, 1951, p. 404.

151 Most evidence suggests that it was the Persians who taught the Jews monotheism when Cyrus the Great defeated Babylonia, where some elements of the Hebrew elite were in captivity. The Persians had been monotheists for almost a thousand years then. This may be why the prophets repeatedly accuse the Jews of worshiping false gods – because they *were* polytheists. Nehemiah and Esdras, sent by Cyrus to Jerusalem to rebuild the city and to spy on Egypt, brought monotheism to Palestine. From the Persians come key concepts in Judaism and Christianity, among them the Messiah (Mehdi in Persian), and also the myth of a virgin being fertilized – a god left his seed in a lake and is waiting for a virgin who will be fertilized when she swims in it.

152 Quoted by Ilan Pappé, Ten Myths of Israel, page 39.

153 Likud is not at all open with information in English, but I could find two versions of the party program available, both reproduced in Appendix II.

154 Nurit Peled-Elhanan (Hebrew University of Jerusalem and David Yellin Teachers College, Israel), *The Representation of 'Others' in Israeli Schoolbooks: A Multimodal Analysis*, CICE Hiroshima University Journal of International Cooperation, Vol. 14, no. 2, 2011, pages 115-130. https://cice.hiroshima-u.ac.jp/wp-content/uploads/2014/03/14-2-8.pdf

155 https://opensiuc.lib.siu.edu/ps_pubs/9/

156 B'tselem, *A regime of Jewish supremacy from the Jordan River to the Mediterranean Sea: This is apartheid*, 2021-01-12, https://www.btselem.org/publications/fulltext/202101_this_is_apartheid

157 Breaking the Silence: *Our Harsh Logic: Israeli Soldiers' Testimonies from the Occupied Territories, 2000-2010*, Metropolitan books, 2012.

158 https://www.breakingthesilence.org.il/about/organization

159 The video can be viewed on the B'tselem website: https://www.btselem.org/ video/20150417_ice_cream_at_hebron_checkpoint

160 Ingmar Carlsson, *Bruden* är *vacker men har redan en man, Sionismen – en ideologi vid vägs* ände?, Wahlström & Widstrand, 2012, page 310.

161 Tomer Persico, *Why religious Zionism is Growing Darker*, Haaretz, 2017-05-17, https://www.haaretz.com/opinion/2017-05-16/ty-article/.premium/why-religious-zionism-isgrowing- darker/0000017f-e13a-d804-ad7f-f1faf5f90000

The complete "Israel's Decisive Plan" can be read on Hashiloach Frontlines: https://hashiloach.org.il/israels-decisive-plan/

162 B'tselem, *The Occupation's Fig Leaf: Israel's Military Law Enforcement System as a Whitewash Mechanism*, https://www.btselem.org/publications/summaries/201605_occupations_fig_leaf

163 Malin Fezehai, *The Disappeared Children of Israel*, The New York Times, 2019-02-20, https://www.nytimes.com/2019/02/20/world/middleeast/israel-yemenite-children-affair.html https://en.wikipedia.org/wiki/Yemenite_Children_Affair

164 See *Demolition and Eviction of Bedouin Citizens of Israel in the Naqab (Negev) - The Prawer Plan*, https://www.adalah.org/en/content/view/7589

165 Zafrir Rinat, *Israel Approves Plans for Four New Jewish Towns in Negev as 'Buffer' Between Bedouin Towns*, Haaretz, 2023-07-31, https://www.haaretz.com/israel-news/2023-07-31/ty-article/.premium/israel-to-approve-plans-for-4-new-jewish-towns-in-negev-as-buffer-betweenbedouin-towns/00000189-ad58-d86a-a1fb-af5eaed50000

166 Jonathan Lis, *Israeli Cabinet Advances Plans to 'Judaize' Galilee, Expand West Bank Settlements*, Haaretz, 2023-06-05, https://www.haaretz.com/israel-news/2023-06-05/ty-article/.premium/israeli-cabinet-advances-plans-to-judaize-galilee-expand-jewish-wb-settlements/00000188-8a67-dded-a58e-abe7a3490000

167 See B'tselem, *East Jerusalem cleansing continues: Israel removes more Palestinian families, hands over their homes to settlers*, 2019.

168 B'tselem, *High Court of Justice paves way for cleansing of Palestinians from Silwan*, 2018.

169 Nurit Peled, op. cit.

170 See Simha Flapan, *The Birth of Israel*. The book is organized in chapters questioning the myths of Zionism. Available online, https://pdfhost.io/v/nRDgxWMUk_The_Birth_of_Israel.pdf.

171 Ilan Pappé, *The ethnic cleansing of Palestine*, Benny Morris, *1948*, among other.

172 Adam Raz, *Classified Docs Reveal Massacres of Palestinians in '48 – and What Israeli Leaders Knew*, Haaretz, 2021-12-09, https://www.haaretz.com/israel-news/2021-12-09/ty-articlemagazine/. highlight/classified-docs-reveal-deir-yassin-massacre-wasnt-the-only-one-perpetratedby-isra/0000017f-e496-d7b2-a77f-e79772340000

173 Ofer Aderet, *State Archive Error Shows Israeli Censorship Guided by Concerns Over National Image*, Haaretz, 2022-01-05, https://www.haaretz.com/israel-news/2022-01-05/ty-article-magazine/. highlight/state-archive-error-shows-israeli-censorship-guided-by-concerns-over-nationalimage/0000017f-f684-d47e-a37f-ffbc1bf50000

174 Jorge Liboreiro, *Josep Borrell apologises for controversial 'garden vs jungle' metaphor but defends speech*, Euronews, 2022-10-19, https://www.euronews.com/my-europe/2022/10/19/josep-borrell-apologises-for-controversial-garden-vs-jungle-metaphor-but-stands-his-ground

175 *WATCH NOW: BEHEADED BABIES AND WOMEN FOUND IN KFAR AZA*, i24News, live 2023-10-10, https://www.youtube.com/watch?v=RKc9ESIEMpw

176 Washington Report on Middle East Affairs, 2015-04-02, *Does Unconditional Support for Israel Endanger Israeli Voices? THE ISRAEL LOBBY—IS IT GOOD FOR THE US?—IS IT GOOD FOR ISRAEL?*, https://www.wrmea.org/the-israel-lobby-is-it-good-for-the-us-is-it-good-for-israel/does-unconditional-support-for-%C2%ADisrael-endanger-israeli-voices.html

177 Gideon Levy went on to show the contradictory nature of Israel's self-image. He quoted Netanyahu: "All Jews must come to Israel. It is the safest place for Jews in the world. It is a protection for the Jews of the world." And continued: "… It was only 24 hours later that [Netanyahu] said that Israel is facing an existential threat because of the Iranian bomb. And I asked myself, how can you dare invite Jews to come and join this suicide project, when the Iranians are going to bomb us?

178 Avram Burg, *The Holocaust is over and we must rise from its ashes*, St. Martin's Griffin, 2012, page 22

179 Burg, op. cit. page 23-24

180 Burg op. cit. page 51

181 Burg, op. cit. page 78

182 Quoted in Ingmar Carlsson, *Bruden* är *vacker men har redan en man, Sionismen – en ideologi vid vägs* ände?, Wahlström & Widstrand, 2012, sidor 175-176.

183 Bergman, op. cit., p. 12.

184 Carlson, op. cit. page 258

185 Theodor Herlz, *The Jewish State*, 1896.

186 Ronny Reyes, *Horrific new stories of Hamas attacks in Israel surface, including rape of 'beautiful woman with face of angel' who screamed to be killed*, New Yoork Post, 2023-12-03.

187 *"A Textbook Case of Genocide": Israeli Holocaust Scholar Raz Segal Decries Israel's Assault on Gaza*, Democracy Now, 2023-10-16, https://www.democracynow.org/2023/10/16/raz_segal_textbook_case_of_genocide

188 The attack also involved the Al-Quds Brigades (belonging to Islamic Jihad) and perhaps the Al-Aqsa Brigades (belonging to al-Fatah) and other groups, but the operation was led by Hamas. In order not to burden the text, I write only Hamas but mean both Hamas men and all others who participated in the attack from the other organized brigades. But the Gazan civilians, armed or not, who crossed to the other side on their own initiative are not included in this concept.

189 Asa Winstanley, *Israeli HQ ordered troops to shoot Israeli captives on 7 October,* The Electronic Intifada, 20 January 2024, https://electronicintifada.net/blogs/asa-winstanley/israeli-hq-ordered-troops-shoot-israeli-captives-7-october. The article of Bergman and Zitun was original published in Ynet: https://w.ynet.co.il/yediot/7-days/time-of-darkness

190 Mark Mazzetti, Ian Austen, Graham Bowley and Malachy Browne, *A Riveting ISIS Story, Told in a Times Podcast, Falls Apart*, The New York Times, 2020-12-18, https://www.nytimes.com/2020/12/18/world/middleeast/caliphate-chaudhry-hoax.html

191 When the Mission of the UN came to Israel they surprisingly did not meet with Dr. Elkayam.Levy. On March 25, 2024, Ali Abunimah wrote in The Electronic Intifada a well documented article that debunk the Civil Commission as a fraud, *Israeli "commission" on 7 October rape claims exposed as fraud*, https://electronicintifada.net/content/israeli-commission-7-october-rape-claims-exposed-fraud/45401

192 *The IDF's Robust System for Operational Conduct*, https://www.youtube.com/watch?v=hOpHUAy-pEIs

193 Alexander Smith, *Information missteps have led to questions about Israel's credibility*, NBC News, 2023-11-18, https://www.nbcnews.com/news/world/information-missteps-led-questions-israels-credibility- rcna125723

194 *Israel-Palestinian conflict: False and misleading claims fact-checked*, BBC, 2021-05-21, https://www.bbc.com/news/57111293

195 Rebecca Rommen, *False claims dead Palestinian baby was 'a doll' go viral on social media in the Israel-Hamas disinformation war*, Business Insider, 2023-12-03, https://www.businessinsider.com/false-claims-dead-palestinian-baby-doll-viral-jerusalem-post-retracts-2023-12?r=US&IR=T

196 *Hasbara Handbook: Promoting Israel on Campus, The World Union of Jewish Students*, 2002, http://www.middle-east-info.org/take/wujshasbara.pdf

197 SVT (Swedish TV, Public Service), *Anders filmed Swedish bunker – used as propaganda in the war*, 2023-12-009, https://www.svt.se/nyheter/lokalt/blekinge/anders-filmade-svensk-bunker-anvands-som- propaganda-by-israel-and-hamas--07ru8f

198 Ilan Pappé, *Ten Myths about Israel*, page 130.

199 Gideon Levy, *When Israel abuses the hostages that it holds*, Haaretz, 2023-12-23 https://www. haaretz.com/opinion/2023-12-23/ty-article/.premium/when-israel-abusesthehostages- that-it-holds/0000018c-97ef-da81-a1bc-dfffe6f80000

200 CBC, *Videos purportedly show 2 Palestinian boys shot dead during Israeli raid in West Bank.* Thomson Reuters Posted: Nov 29, 2023, https://www.cbc.ca/news/world/west-bank-palestinian-boys-shot-1.7044430

201 Yael Hallak, *What Happened on October 7 Humiliated Israeli Masculinity. The Response Is Violence*, 2023-12-15, https://www.haaretz.com/israel-news/2023-12-15/ty-article-magazine/.highlight/what-happened-on-october-7-humiliated-israeli-masculinity-the-response-is-violence/0000018c-68bb-de43-affd-fcbb5fe40000

202 Yossi Melman, *'The Misconception Was That the Palestinians Aren't a People. They're Willing to Kill and Be Killed for Their Independence'*, 2024-01-10, https://www.haaretz.com/israel-news/ 2024-01-10/ty-article-magazine/.premium/the-misconception-was-that-the-palestinians-arent-apeople/0000018c-eec3-d0b4-a7ce-ffe38ec80000

203 See "British Holocaust Denial in Embryo" by Alexander Ratcliffe in Holocaust and Genocide Denial: A Contextual Perspective by Mark Hobbs, Taylor & Francis, 2017, p. 16.

204 "Why 'murder of babies' is the pinnacle of war propaganda" by Nusmila Lohani, The Business Standard, November 2, 2023. https://www.tbsnews.net/features/panorama/why-murder-babies-pinnacle-war-propaganda-731582.

205 Ibid.

206 Ibid.

207 "Fake news banade väg för kaos i Mellanöstern" by Patrik Paulov and Per Shapiro in Svenska Dagbladet, 2020-10-09. https://www.svd.se/a/rgAnRm/fake-news-banade-vag-for-kaos-i-mellanostern